CHURCHES OF FRANCE

THE MACMILLAN COMPANY
NEW YORK · BOSTON · CHICAGO · DALLAS
ATLANTA · SAN FRANCISCO

MACMILLAN & CO., Limited
LONDON · BOMBAY · CALCUTTA
MELBOURNE

THE MACMILLAN COMPANY
OF CANADA, Limited
TORONTO

John Taylor Arms - 1923

PARIS

THE "PENSEUR DE NOTRE DAME"

Size of the original etching, 12⅜ inches by 9 15/16 inches

CHURCHES OF FRANCE

TEXT BY DOROTHY NOYES ARMS
WITH FIFTY-ONE REPRODUCTIONS
OF ETCHINGS AND DRAWINGS
BY JOHN TAYLOR ARMS

THE MACMILLAN COMPANY
NEW YORK   MCMXXIX

COMPOSITION BY J. S. CUSHING CO.
PRINTED IN THE UNITED STATES OF AMERICA BY BERWICK & SMITH

TO OUR MOTHERS

1929

TO MESSRS. KENNEDY AND COMPANY ARE DUE OUR
APPRECIATIVE THANKS FOR PERMISSION TO USE THE
ETCHINGS AND DRAWINGS REPRODUCED IN THIS VOLUME.

FOREWORD

It is axiomatic that each individual sees an object, hears a story, or remembers an incident in his own way, which varies — sometimes to a considerable extent—from the vision, the hearing, or the memory of every other person involved. Yet each is right. Our personalities change the outlines of an experience as our physical eyes see things, large or small, clear or cloudy, according to the individual vision.

Every country has a special message for every one of us, and there is no standardizing them, nor need of it. When I write of France, it is from a personal point of view, based on our own experiences and on our own reactions to them. At one end of the scale is the pure exquisiteness of Gothic architecture carried to unbelievable beauty, and at the other end the little, simple contacts and incidents of everyday life. The extremes, and all the intermediate points, make up the full richness and flavor of the whole. Each new episode adds its spice or aroma, each new revealing of individual or national characteristics adds the mellowness of deepened sympathy.

France is very dear to us. We have been, perhaps, unusually fortunate in the glimpses permitted us into the various strata of French life. We have lived enough months there to penetrate a little bit into the meanings of things, under the distractingly interesting surface, and we have always been in sympathy with the country and its people. To us France is like one of its famous wines, full of age and flavor; into the making of each went rain and cold winds as well as brilliant sunshine, weary toil as well as the spirit of joyous creation, coöperation, individual effort and, perhaps most of all, the richness due to years. To fully appreciate either, one needs an abundance of leisure, sympathy and the understanding of that old-world patience which counts time as naught.

CONTENTS

CONTENTS

ILLUSTRATIONS

ILLUSTRATIONS

[xiv]

ILLUSTRATIONS

CHURCHES OF FRANCE

PARIS

TO each age its compensations. In the days before trains, when one went afoot or on horseback, the conservative must have regarded the advent of the iron monsters of steam with regret, as a mechanical innovation which would soon rob travel of its pleasure. Later, the bicycle too was looked upon askance as affording such an easy method of transportation between places that the individual characteristics of each town would soon become blurred. The arrival of the automobile was heralded as a sure means of ruining the local color of places by bringing distant points so much nearer together. And we of this day, who love the different quality of other lands, regard the use of the aeroplane in daily life with disfavor and distrust. Already the boundaries of the world have shrunk unbelievably. When we fly casually and easily there will be no unknown territory left and the fascination of mystery will have gone. There is no doubt that this is a matter for regret in many ways. Modern Alexanders must weep for lack of lands to conquer, but as we find ourselves unable to alter conditions we must adjust our minds to things as they are and so we shall discover in them unthought-of beauties and compensations.

Things change inevitably with increased intercourse between people, due to better means of transportation and easier exchange of ideas through the newspapers, the radio and what not. With this goes a tendency to standardization; the peasants of to-day, for instance, have rejected the colorful costume of their ancestors and have clad themselves enthusiastically in the cheap, efficient, ugly garb of modern times. The world has lost beauty thereby but individuals have often gained a bodily freedom, a safeguarding of health, which the picturesque costumes, handed down from generation to generation, did not ensure. Yet there is a definite tendency now to revive the use of the old-time habiliments for state occasions. If this continues, we shall see the best adjustment of the question possible in this modern workaday world — efficiency for the days of labor, beauty for the feast days.

And so it is with other things. Superstitions — interesting to the outsider as typifying some local legend, perhaps, but destructive to live with — melt away as horizons broaden: local vanities soften with the knowledge of other places and things, but most important of all, prejudices between individuals, between cities, between countries, soften with the greater knowledge gained of the problems, the failures, the aspirations and the friendliness of others. Trust between two people springs most of all from understanding, and so it is with nations. That which we lose in picturesqueness, we gain in sympathy, and that which we gain in sympathy makes for international harmony and good will.

We have traveled by train and we have traveled by motor, and though we have often wished that we might have the best of the past added to the best of the present, yet I think we of to-day have gained as much as we have lost. After all, the adventure of voyaging is mental in its essence rather than physical, and it now takes a subtler appreciation to savor it most thoroughly but the joy is there as fully as it was even twenty years ago, if one brings to it the proper equipment of enthusiasm and interest.

NOTRE DAME DE PARIS

PHYSICALLY and spiritually the cathedral of Notre Dame is the center of Paris. From my first knowledge of it, when as a child of ten I looked with caught breath and fascinated eyes at the immensity of its almost terrifying interior, then fled to the comforting sight of busy human life along the nearby quays, until now, when uncounted hours of adult appreciation have served to make of this cathedral not a thing to be seen and thought about but rather a part of myself, a consciousness of something too immense wholly to grasp, it has seemed the most significant point in that city. The roots of it go so deep into the history of France and the love of the French people, it is so inextricably a part of them as a nation, that it is their very heart. The Seine — that great artery of commerce — bathes its foundations, wide streets and avenues teeming with life encircle it close at hand though keeping a respectful distance; the Conciergerie, the Palais de Justice, the Hôtel de Ville, the old, old town from which sprang this far-reaching city of modern Paris, all are nearby, under the wide protecting influence of this cathedral of supreme dignity.

There are many churches in France dedicated to the Virgin, more than to any saint, yet when one speaks of Notre Dame one thinks first of this one in Paris. One feels in it not the young Mary whom life had touched magically, and who must have lived for many years in a state of spiritual, uplifted happiness, hardly believing in her destiny, and only haunted at times by vague, dis-

PARIS

NOTRE DAME DE PARIS

Size of the original etching, 12¼ inches by 14 inches

John Taylor Arms - 1925

PARIS

THE SOUTH TRANSEPT OF NOTRE DAME, SEEN FROM THE RUE SAUTON

Size of the original etching, 1½ inches by 7½ inches

John Taylor Arms 1924

quieting fears; not that Mary, but the anguished mother who had lived through unbelievable agony, whose love and faith had been put to the severest test, yet who had come through with her belief unclouded and her heart untinged with bitterness. She is the great mother with mature maternal mind, whose sympathizing love goes out to all mankind with a deep and understanding fervor born of her own first-hand knowledge of supreme suffering and sacrifice.

This cathedral is so well known that any description of it is superfluous. It is ancient, so much so that its roots go back to the beginnings of Paris, yet it is perennially new in appeal. Less graceful, less finely beautiful than those of Chartres and Amiens, it has a personality which yields first place to none. It should be seen, not once, but countless times until it becomes a composite thing in one's mind, made up of memories of sun and rain, of weather-pocked stone, of sculptures so human they seem alive, of carved portals so deep the shadows cast are almost tangible, of vast dark vistas in the interior where giant windows cast jeweled patterns of color on historic walls and chanting voices echo back from lost spaces. One must remember ghosts; that of the English Henry who was made King of France here in 1431, of Mary Stuart crowned as beautiful queen consort of Francis II, and of Esmeralda and Quasimodo, no less real because they lacked physical being — their spirits haunt the towers with a living tragedy. Even quite modern ghosts lurk in the dim corners of the great interior; the bloody memory of the Reign of Terror, the overweening ambition of Napoleon whose coronation is almost legendary now, the sad spirit of the other Napoleon and his lovely empress, and sometimes, when all is very quiet, one can hear a faint whir of wings, and a pale wraith of an aeroplane hovers for a moment over the cathedral.

We usually remember a well-loved, well-known place under some particular condition of light, and Notre Dame shows me four distinct faces in my mental picture gallery. One of the loveliest and least known views is that to be had from the nearby garden of St. Julien-le-Pauvre. This tiny ancient church contests with St. Germain des Prés the right to call itself the oldest in Paris; it certainly gives the appearance of greater age. St. Julien was a wealthy and thoughtless youth, fond of hunting. A wounded stag was given speech one day, and prophesied that he would become a patricide. He scoffed at the idea but later, through a terrible combination of circumstances, he did kill his parents, then, realizing the truth of the prophecy, he became converted to a life of poverty. He dedicated himself to the poor and died a leper, and he is

[5]

the particular patron saint of minstrels. It seems fitting that his church should be small, obscure and poor and situated in the Latin quarter among the minstrels — if one may call them that — of modern times. Into the neglected garden, where a Roman wall bears mute witness to antiquity, we went one fall day to see Notre Dame and add another phase of its personality to our composite memory. The grass rustled dryly as we passed and the last leaves on the straggling bushes whispered with parched voices in the faint breeze. The cathedral rose before us a beautiful mass, its outlines faintly blurred and softened by what could hardly be called a haze, rather the impalpable, barely visible blueness of an autumn day.

The magnificent apse is so beautiful that I hardly like to express even a seasonal preference, yet I remember it with especial joy when a light fall of snow had blanketed Paris in white purity. The wet stone seemed darker, the snow whiter, when contrasted one with the other, and the striking silhouette of that remarkable architectural achievement was even more obvious. The airy quality of the great buttresses which vault across such wide spaces was accentuated, while losing nothing of structural solidity. The tapering apse rose with even greater majesty in somber outline against the gray sky.

Our feet have taken their slight toll from the stone treads of the spiral stairway which leads up to the towers. What thoughtful or heedless, what famous or unknown, what joyous or sad steps have served to wear away that resisting material into such treacherous slants and unsuspected hollows! We had waited for a day of brilliant sunshine on which to make this particular pilgrimage and we were well rewarded. We came out upon the upper gallery and found ourselves surrounded by familiar sights — grotesques, animals, chimeras, things to dream about, and all of them as well-known as friendly faces. Below us lay the city, melting imperceptibly into the country through its outlying suburbs. The river intersected it with sharp precision; the boulevards radiated in starlike lines; Sacré Cœur raised a distant head and St. Jacques a nearer tower; each miniature house was distinct and clear, the similarity insisted on by Baron Haussmann which should have been tedious was in fact pleasing; only the old-time section was a formless mass. The white fleecy clouds of a windy, sun-drenched day trailed dark shadow patches across the wide-flung city.

The gardienne took us under her immediate and personal protection the instant the drawing-board came into view. Was she not the hereditary protector of this history-soaked spot? Father and son, they had guarded the tower

PARIS

GARGOYLE STUDIES

Size of the original etching, 3 inches by 2¼ inches

John Taylor Arms - 1924

until, helas! there was no son and so she, daughter though she was, had inherited the position. Monsieur loved the gargoyles? Ah, Monsieur had an eye for beauty! They were not the funny things to laugh at that the blind pigs of tourists so often thought them. No! They were human, tragic, what you will, but never, never a joke. Ah, Monsieur loved the works of Meryon? There was a man! Had she not often heard her father speak of him, how he came day by day to draw the Stryge or the belfry, when often *le pauvre* had difficulty getting up the stairs, so weak was he from hunger. But so proud, no one must guess, or help him.

She took us through locked gates to see yet more grotesques usually unseen by the casual visitor, and she took us into the belfry, a place for haunted dreams. Here the great struts support the interior and make a framework capable of holding the immense weight of the bells. They cross and recross in a pattern of line which is disturbingly beautiful. Bright sunlight streams through chinks in the walls making ribbons of brilliant gold, the shadows are black and the great beams look oppressively heavy. One needs a steady head and a quiet mind, or somber ghosts crowd in and fill the belfry with thought and sound.

The façade is most poignant to me in a fine rain. The streets shine and reflect long lines of things on the shimmering pavements; the yellow lamps hardly relieve the gloom but look like spots of color in the thick, heavy air; the great cathedral rises to endless heights, and the truncated towers seem to carry on indefinitely, veiled as their summits are in wreathing mist. One feels the upward lift, the vertical line which never stops.

We were in Paris during the flood of the Seine in January 1924. For years the river had been peaceful and had run a docile, well-trained way between the masonry banks, but this fall was wet; rain fell and yet more rain, until the spongy ground could hold no more. Then a sudden thaw melted distant mountain snows and added the water thus released to the swollen brooks and streams. These in turn poured their redoubled selves into the burdened rivers and the captive Seine began to rise, steadily, inexorably. At first it seemed a newspaper affair, there was so little evidence of the subterranean floods already under way. We read accounts of cellars where stored furniture floated on the mounting tide, of others whose heavier contents lay submerged and ruined beyond hope. Then we began to see the signs of the times along the river banks.

[7]

Low-lying quays were covered little by little, inch by inch, their heaped-up piles of cement or sand sucked away and adding their quota of opaque color to the swirling yellow waters. The boats ceased moving and strained heavily at the ropes which held them to the sides; the arches of the bridges, usually high enough for most of the river craft save those tugs and launches which must fold back their funnels in order to pass beneath them, began to show smaller and smaller openings through which the boiling torrent forced an angry way. Higher and higher on the walls mounted the line of flood, and crowds of people stood in the mist and rain watching the unchecked rise with a certain fatalistic resignation. There was talk of blasting the Pont d'Alma to relieve the congestion caused by its narrow span. It seemed a pagan offering of this historic bridge to an insatiable monster. The Metropolitain became a weird place with whole stations closed to the public, or temporary passageways built away from the spots where the greatest quantity of water dripped from overhead or oozed through the side walls. High overshoes were as necessary underground as above; so were umbrellas, only the cramped space did not permit of their use, and one added one's personal sacrifice of a hat to the demands of the greedy flood, wondering as one watched the water gathering fast in pools whether the curving roof would give way and human life now, as of old, would be needed to satisfy a cruel craving.

It was an eerie time, with the streets strange and unfriendly. The buildings were half hidden by a dirty brown fog which necessitated lights on cars and in the streets, even at noonday. Everything was wet, and indoors it was little better; the dampness and mist crept in through every crack and entered boldly when a door was opened even for a moment. Things were blanketed by moisture, dulled by wetness. Services were being held in all the churches with special appeals that the danger would go no farther but might stop while the damage was yet slight. All day long there was heard the ceaseless muffled thud of the leather-covered doors through which came the devout to say their personal prayer for their beloved city, or for the safety of their homes if, perchance, they were dwellers by the river.

Life seemed to go on much as usual on the surface, but each of us carried a subconscious load of apprehension. As things grew worse this feeling deepened, and one day, in that restless, aimless mood which a chronic worry engenders in me, I turned my steps towards Notre Dame, the most comforting church in Paris, hoping for a good omen. The vast interior seemed yet more immense in the velvety blackness. The bright points of light stabbing it barely

[8]

John Taylor Arms, 1923.

relieved the gloom. The nave was well filled with kneeling figures and each chapel had its group of supplicants, varying in size according to the popularity of the particular saint to whom the altar was dedicated. Mass was going on and the brilliantly illuminated altar appeared to glow with a more fervent light, the invocations seemed even more intense than usual. The very atmosphere was charged with a feeling of throbbing tension and ardor. My awaited message was not to be found there, and I left by the door in the great west façade. The rain had stopped for a moment and the fog was lifting. I could see the square massive towers high above me which lately had been so often veiled from view. They were strong, majestic, sublime, and they calmed my little human fears by their supreme dignity. They had seen everything in their life through the centuries — the height and depth of human development, the best and worst work of the elements, and all the shifting kaleidoscopic drama of the years. They were the spirit of Notre Dame, the sorrowing mother who gives her children comfort in their troubles because, no matter how great their tragedy, hers was so infinitely greater. Her cathedral has that same power for me. I went away renewed in courage, knowing that this troubled moment, which seemed so important to us, was but a breath upon the waters to this understanding church which has presided so serenely all these years over her well-loved city.

ST. GERMAIN L'AUXERROIS

HOW poignantly some small detail may recall a place, a person or an experience. It is true that a photograph of St. Germain l'Auxerrois can give me its physical aspects perfectly; it can refresh my mind so that it appreciates anew the dignity of the design and the sumptuousness of the detail, but let me get one whiff of a newly sprinkled dusty street and instantly I am back in memory to the moment when I first saw and loved this gentle church.

Summer had descended upon Paris with a suddenness and a completeness which left its population literally gasping for breath. The little round tables of the cafés were filled, from the outermost edges of the sidewalks to the cool, dim depths of the inner rooms, by people endeavoring to replenish the moisture which the heat was steadily and surely drawing from every pore. The Rivoli arcades were crowded with perspiring humanity growling or shrilling over the weather according to their varying temperaments and vocal chords.

I left the comparative comfort of this shade and crossed a street full of dancing lights, where every windshield and every bit of polished metal reflected the merciless sunshine and added unbearably to the glare. The great gray arches of the Louvre offered a momentary respite before I stepped into the empty brilliance of the paved court beyond. Then came another arch and another street of clanging tramcars until I found myself in a tiny *place* where a few people dozed on benches under the drooping trees, a cabman slept on the box of his fiacre while his horse, with hanging head, seemed turned to stone. From behind and from either side came the ceaseless hum of a noisy city, but here all was quiet and remote. A watering cart had just passed, leaving in its wake the pungent odor of damp dust so characteristic of Paris. Before me rose the church, aloof, exquisite, so far above the fret and worry of a workaday world and so untroubled and serene, that the heat and hurry of the day fell away from me and I went in through the deep portal refreshed and comforted in body and in spirit.

Perhaps this is the loveliest of all the churches dedicated to St. Germain of Auxerre. It has always seemed to me one of the aristocrats of French Gothic. There is a quality of exquisiteness, of high-bred reserve which suggests a Grande Dame of the olden days. St. Germain des Prés, which resembles it only in name, is the militant church, the manly warrior, while Notre Dame seems always the sorrowing mother who stretches out loving arms to her sinning children. But this church, great lady in quality that it is, has a different personality and a different appeal. It is sympathetic, but rather with the intellectual and spiritual ills of humanity than with its cruder and more brutal sins. I think a murderer could more easily confess his crime at Notre Dame than here. I was interested to find out that history bears out my personal feeling. This was the parish church of the Bourbon family and has always been associated so closely with royalty that it is not to be wondered at if even the stones have arrogated to themselves a regal feeling.

The exterior is even finer and more distinctive than the interior. The mellow, crumbling porch and gracious portal have always been a beauty spot which I trust the hand of the restorer, now at work, will deal with gently. The belfry, built apart from the church itself, is the most unusual feature and the finest. In shape it suggests a miniature Tour St. Jacques, but there the resemblance ceases. It is such a mass of open work, of windows and tiny flying buttresses, canopies and gargoyles, that one is forced to the obvious comparison with a piece of jewelry. The best view is from the court between the north wall of the church and the nearby Mairie. From here I was able to

PARIS

SENTINELS

Size of the original etching, 4⅛ inches by 7¼ inches

John Taylor Arms

get an excellent idea of the structure of the church, of the lovely balustrade around its roof and light buttresses terminating in very attenuated, highly fantastic water spouts. The silhouette of the tower is especially fine from this side, and the large flanking angels build up to it well.

St. Germain claims the doubtful honor of having rung the bell which ushered in the Massacre of St. Bartholomew. It was hard to believe, as I stood in that remote and peaceful courtyard looking at the exquisite delicacy and proud outline of the unusual tower, that anything so lovely could have stooped to such an act. What scenes of horror and bloodshed to be ushered in by the seeming innocence of a church bell, its chime tolled backwards! What a blot on French and churchly history! As I stood there thinking of that terrible night the carillon above my head suddenly pealed out the hour of noon, its gay notes lending an eerie reality to my somber thoughts.

The interior is much less beautiful. It has been drastically restored with indifferent success, most noticeably in the choir. The general feeling of color is lovely; the undecorated walls and masonry are uniformly gray, pure, luminous and quite pale. In this neutral pallor the apsidal windows glow intensely. There seems to be considerable difference of opinion as to the date of these; those in the transepts are authentic sixteenth century but these of the apse are under discussion. Some say seventeenth century, but local pride claims fourteenth and points to the ancient Breton costumes depicted in each as proof positive that they really were given by the Duchess Anne, that remarkable woman who holds the unique honor of having been married to two French kings. Her union, first with Charles IX and then with his cousin and successor Louis XI, joined her great duchy of Brittany finally and completely to the crown of France. Possibly these mooted windows were her gift, but the needed restorations have left so little of the original glass, while still keeping the designs, as to make both opinions correct. They are less mellow, perhaps, than the others, but they make a gorgeous blaze of color at the end of a stretch of almost uninterrupted grayness.

Against the wall of the choir is built an upper room, the private pew of Louis XVI and his beautiful, ill-fated queen. Through the dim glass of the casements behind which they sat when they came to church, one can see the rich ruby coloring of the windows beyond and the gilded crowns carved upon the ceiling, a vivid symbol of their martyrdom. A secret tunnel, with triple iron gates of complicated locks, connected this room with the Tuileries. They left their palace by this furtive underground route fearing hostile demonstrations on the part of the people whom they governed. Yet all their precautions failed, where courage and a better understanding of conditions might have saved them their throne and certainly their lives. I wonder what they thought of, poor tragic pair, in this high retreat of theirs. I am sure that he, so good, so stupid, so misplaced, followed the service with his kind heart and middle class mind on it, while she, beautiful, brilliant and thoughtless, listened but half attentively, solacing herself with dreams of still greater glory or torturing herself with vain longings for things which neither her exalted position nor her boundless extravagance could attain. But later, when months of imprisonment and a suffering-inspired knowledge of human nature as it really is, not as it looks to kings, had taught her truer understanding, when widowed and bereft of earthly comforts, then she turned instinctively and sincerely to her religion. And it was the courageous curé of St. Germain l'Auxerrois who, braving public sentiment, visited her in the Conciergerie during her incarceration, and at the end carried and administered to her there the last sacraments of the church.

The final gift from royalty to this favored church is a charming baptismal font in the southern transept. Designed by Mme. Lamartine, it was presented by Napoleon Bonaparte when his small son was christened here. The marble was quarried in Italy, as the sacristan proudly informed me, and the workmen were Romans, because the child, poor little King of Rome, had been destined by his empire-seeking father to rule one day in the Eternal City.

And so, from its beginnings until the end of a monarchy in France, St. Germain l'Auxerrois has been a royal church. The kings are gone and their pomp and panoply is a dream only to be seen in the dusty sadness of museums, but at night, I am sure, regal ghosts come back to this historic spot of memories to relive a little of their vanished glory.

ABBEVILLE

I FEEL that I can never be entirely fair to Abbeville; it has a place in my affections quite out of proportion to its architectural rating, interesting though that is, and it all came about this way.

We had both known and loved France with the careless point of view of youth: it was a place of beauty, of quaint foreignness, to look at, to enjoy on the surface of things and to leave. Then came a period of personal responsibilities, then the war, and when in 1923 we set sail for our first European adventure together, it was with mixed feelings of pleasant anticipations and misgivings. Four years, the most cataclysmic known to mankind, had brought undreamed-of changes to the whole world. It was older and sadder, if not wiser, and we ourselves had aged far more than the counted time. What would France be like? Would the tragedy through which it had passed, and the inevitable scars which could never quite be healed, so overshadow the land that the joyousness would have gone out of it? Could one smile in that war-tormented country, or would it be merely a place of death? Such questions bothered us as we landed, and though Paris at first sight seemed much the same, the real test could only come in the provinces.

We reached Abbeville, our first appointed stop, one sunny day of early July. Busy people were hurrying about the streets, the clack of wooden shoes alternating with the pound of almost equally hard leather; the little shops were open and doing a thriving trade and groups formed at street corners to argue or laugh together as they have done since time immemorial. No one but ourselves appeared to notice the wrecked houses here and there, mute witnesses of attacks by air. Abbeville was a normal, brisk French town going on its usual way. We realized then that France — gallant spirit that she is — was carrying on in spite of her mortal scars, and that so long as the race exists it will keep its priceless heritage of enjoyment. Because Abbeville demonstrated that to us more vividly than any explanation could have done, it has a permanent and special place in our affections.

It is a lovely town, besides — compact, snug and picturesque. The Somme divides it almost in half, flowing swiftly where it is tight pent between ancient houses whose cellar walls are canal banks for its guidance. From an overhanging window of one of these we were amused to see a projecting fishing-rod, the tempting bait upon the extremity of its line far below it in the fast running water. Having since watched the patient Frenchmen fish, I realize that this untended pole was merely an optimistic gesture, rather than a real hope. How they fish, and fish, and fish, and if perchance one succeeds in capturing a finny prize it proves to be a wriggling minnow four or five inches long. His envious companions cast down their unproductive rods and cluster about him, congratulating him with a fervor only increased by the green-eyed demon of jealousy. They weigh it speculatively in hands unaccustomed to the task, they examine the winning hook, and discuss the bait with fervent interest. The lucky man may never succeed again, but he does not need to, he is a marked soul for life. So even the Abbeville fishing-rod was a symbol of the unchanged nature of the true Frenchman.

Every hour of our stay was an adventure of discovery. The hotel proved a treasure of picturesqueness and amusing contrasts. We entered under an upper room flung across space like a bridge, into an inner court where a fountain bubbled with cool splashing noises over bottles of wine and mineral water stacked for chilling in the basin. From one side a spiral staircase mounted to the rooms which opened off its curving walls at odd and unexpected angles. On the other side, next to the office, a ground-glass door proclaimed itself as the Salle des Bains. It housed a dingy tub which (when a guest with sufficient temerity asked for a bath) was filled by pails of hot water brought from the nearby kitchen. Later a soapy stream rushed forth into the court, wetting the feet of the unsuspecting bystander. Things being so primitive, we expected a small and crowded dining-room, but were ushered instead into a great hall of faded splendor; a velvet seat ran the length and breadth of it, shrouded chandeliers hung from the ceiling, and painted walls, mirror-hung, completed the picture. This was a last relic of former gaiety of the days when Abbeville was the great center of the linen trade. It is still a town of textile workers; the factories get their power from the river, and produce, among other things, the heavy linen sheets which even the comparatively poor still use. They despise our affection for cotton however fine, they feel that only pure linen, though it may be as coarse and uncongenial as sailcloth, is fit covering for any bed.

The little city is closely built about its central cathedral dedicated to St. Vulfran. He was an inconspicuous early martyr who brought Christianity to this place, who founded its first church and who was buried in it. His reliquary may still be seen, and the building is full of sculpture, paintings and glass,

PARIS

ST. GERMAIN L'AUXERROIS

Size of the original etching, 9⅞ inches by 4⅞ inches

SAINT GERMAIN L'AUXERROIS

John Taylor Arms · 1928.

whose subject-matter recalls many incidents in the life of this well loved but little known saint.

The cathedral is quite late, in fact it was only finished in the fifteenth century, and there is about it still an incompleted air, due, I suppose, to the lack of harmony between the nave and façade. The latter is quite lovely, Flamboyant in feeling, but the church as a whole is not particularly satisfactory. In fact it was so much less interesting to me than the personality of the town that it made only a slight impression, and my mental picture is confined largely to the one famous view of it from the Place Admiral Courbet. It is short, compared to its height, and it peers over the peaked roofs and gables of the old houses lining the square with a gay and saucy air. The never-completed tower seems a jaunty cap set askew, and one feels affection for it rather than awe.

There is a café at one corner of this open "place" from which is to be had the one perfect sight of the cathedral. Countless artists must come, as we did, with the firm determination that, come what may, the one viewpoint not to be selected is the one which shows the nave and tower above that frieze of picturesque houses. We succumbed, as have all the others apparently, it is so much the loveliest, really the only composition worth recording. Half-ashamed, we installed ourselves at a little table which a few francs made ours for the day, or for the week for that matter, and while J. T. began the drawing the friendly proprietor stood about and told us tales of the bombardment of 1918, stories of the English whose base this was during the war and anecdotes of the endless procession of artists who sat at that selfsame table to draw that selfsame subject.

As I look back, I remember best the town, gay, gallant and busy about its affairs. The church is lovely, but it seems somehow a little incidental, the spirit of Abbeville is the outstanding feature.

AMIENS

WE journeyed to Amiens one summer day, when J. T. was to renew his acquaintance with its famous cathedral and I was to see it for the first time. It was hot, with the well-nigh unbearable heat which comes to France during the first two weeks of July and which breaks with a complete suddenness on the fourteenth or thereabouts. It is as if there were some strange analogy between the elements and those troublous days of 1789, when excitement ran fever-high and bodies and souls burned with an unabating fire. The human crisis gathered momentum and broke in a first fury with the taking of the Bastille; now Nature celebrates the day with a violent storm. But there the comparison ceases, there is no resemblance between the succeeding Reign of Terror, with its passions and cruelties, and the cool summer of gentle showers and soft sunshine.

We found Amiens a busy, thriving city with modern streets and houses, but scarred here and there by gaping open stretches where destructive bombs had fallen. We hurried to see the cathedral, eager for our first glimpse, and anticipating any number of viewpoints to tempt the pencil. We found it so surpassingly beautiful that it took us time to realize the utter incongruity of its setting. There is that exquisite façade, in which perfection of design and exquisiteness of workmanship are carried to a superlative degree, and with a balance so subtle that it is like the hair-fine adjustment of a delicate instrument; yet all this beauty rises from a plain paved square, closed in dully by rows of featureless houses which seem to turn blank, unseeing eyes upon the loveliness of the church.

Unaided by any graciousness of surroundings the façade of Amiens is so beautiful that nothing can detract from it, but the problem of the artist becomes more difficult. We walked those glaring, unshaded streets for hours in search of a subject. From every corner the slender spires and high roof of the cathedral beckoned alluringly, but always in the foreground were ugly buildings whose uncompromising modern lines cut harshly into the Gothic mass beyond. Only the Basse Ville remained and thither we turned our steps. The streets grew narrow; roofs began to project at pleasantly acute angles above our heads; unsafe, unhealthy houses, which sagged charmingly, began to be

ABBEVILLE
ST. VULFRAN
Size of the original etching, 7½ inches by 7¾ inches

John Taylor Arms 1925

more frequent and countless little canals ran under us or served as watery highways. From them rose a mixed odor of which each component part was a dreadful thing and which united into a whole so evil that it seemed almost tangible.

It is a family saying that J. T. only begins to feel interested in looking for a subject when the air becomes foul, so inextricably are picturesqueness and dirt combined; I was hardly surprised therefore to have him choose the bank of one of the worst of the canals where, moreover, there was no shade, not an hour's respite from the merciless sun. But there was a view, one which he felt sure no one had ever found before him. There was a bridge from door to street, gabled houses and above them the exquisite church of a fairylike delicacy. It made a faultless composition, though his feeling of discovery was crushed when he saw, months later, several etchings made from the identical corner.

How the kindly inhabitants of the quarter worried about him! They begged him, singly and in groups, to stop, to come in out of the sun if only for a few minutes; they brought him water which he dared not drink and umbrellas which they longed to hold over his bent head. Towards the end of the second day a cooling breeze sprang up, and feeling in uplifted mood, J. T. (in whose makeup an ear for music is distinctly absent, but who, nevertheless, loves to sing) burst into triumphant song. He did not notice the presence of two unobtrusive small boys watching him until he overheard one say to the other, imagining him to be a foreigner with no knowledge of French, "You know he draws better than he sings, that man." Their consternation when he laughed and agreed with them can only be imagined by one with a knowledge of the innate, instinctive courtesy of the French.

I found two features very surprising in this Cathedral of Notre Dame, its size and the quality of the light in the interior. The proportions are so perfect, the scale so fine that my mental picture of it, based largely on photographs, was of a moderately large building, while in reality most authorities call it the largest church in France. It is vast, and it looks even vaster, especially in the interior where the simple piers carry up and up in unbroken lines to dim delicate groining. Yet it lives in my memory not for its size but for its supreme beauty and restraint.

With my eyes accustomed to Paris churches and those of the south, whose interiors are characterized by mysterious gloom, the pale color and clear strong light of this cathedral of Amiens was a distinct surprise. At first I missed the half-seen detail, the shadowy vista where my imagination could supply the missing parts at will, then, as I grew used to the uncompromising illumination I realized that only a supremely beautiful edifice could afford such revealment. This interior has nothing to conceal, everything to show, and it can well dispense with the kindly half-lights which lend fictitious beauty to less perfect churches. A faultless face, a pure soul and a great building need no veil of shadow — the clustered piers, the graceful vaulting and the harmonious detail of Notre Dame d'Amiens can only gain by being wholly seen.

We climbed the tower together one afternoon and looked down upon that great nave, with scars from bombs still visible. More fortunate than Rheims and with more time in which to prepare for this contingency, the authorities had all the beautiful glass removed, crated and stored during the war period, so that they lost none of this irreplaceable treasure and except for the slight surface damage to the roof, the church suffered no injury at all. The work of removing the windows was done by members of the fire department, which seemed odd until we realized that they not only have the necessary long ladders but are the most unoccupied class in France. Who ever heard of a French fire in modern days, or has so much as seen an engine on the streets? They also replaced it, I believe, though on this my first visit there only a little of it was installed; the rest, still in its wooden cases, waited in the aisles.

Around the tower and from the eaves of the roof we studied the gargoyles, identifying the ones which J. T. had drawn on a trip to this, his first French cathedral, a number of years before. About the church lay the busy town of modern houses and here and there an empty stretch or a gap of tumbled ruins where ill-aimed bombs had struck perilously near. Still lower was the old quarter where J. T. had been drawing, a city in itself with its own customs and manners and people, quite distinct and apart from their more modern neighbours. In the heart of this was the church of St. Leu, as old and picturesque as the quarter itself and with a quality of venerable tolerance.

In the distance we could see the Somme and the fertile valley land which, with its many counterparts in this river-watered country of Normandy, make it the dairy spot of France. It is a region of green fields, of fat, well-cared-for cattle and of rich milk, which they thoroughly skim in order that extra butter may be made. They sell the pale blue residue as whole milk and babies drink it and stay thin — no wonder! The food laws are still in a very embryonic stage in this otherwise highly civilized country.

When we had asked if we might climb the tower the custodian, being busy, had sent us up alone with instructions that when we descended we were to ring

THE CATHEDRAL OF NOTRE DAME, FROM THE LOWER TOWN

Size of the original etching, 10½ inches by 6¾ inches

John Taylor Arms. 1926.

a bell which we would find near the foot of the stairs, and he would let us out. We entered from the outside of the church and were to emerge by a different way directly into the aisle, so that it was not until we had groped a hesitating way down the last dim stairs that we realized he had omitted to tell us exactly where the bell was located. We fumbled about and came upon no trace of it, we searched diligently in every pocket for the matches which are always there and this time were not, we felt the walls again and yet again until finally, realizing that closing time must be fast approaching, we beat upon that stout oak door with the strength of despair. There are many things worse than spending a night locked into one of the most beautiful monuments of the world, but there are certain distinct disadvantages to it also. It was bound to be cold and, worse than that, I anticipated rats, a thought which redoubled my efforts. We could hear people on the other side of that impenetrable barrier, human happy people who were going home to hot dinners and comfortable beds, but they either did not hear us or put our racket down to the hammering of carpenters at work upon some necessary repairs. We had about decided that we really were there for the night and that shortly we would climb again at least to enjoy the oncoming sunset and evening light across the city, when we heard approaching footsteps and a very irate gardien appeared, growling gruffly about people who stayed away so long and who had no consideration for other people's dinner hour. We quickly and meekly emerged without a word and with only one backward glance in search of that mythical bell. There it hung upon the wall; our hands must have been within an inch of it many times but never quite near enough. We came out of the blackness into the vast awe-inspiring nave and there, upon the pure, pale pillars and upon the pavement worn by pious or beauty-seeking footsteps of countless generations, the late sun, streaming through the western rose, made dazzling jeweled patterns of blue and red and gold.

So far to the north the days were long at this midsummer time, and when their hurry and business were over we went out in the evenings to explore the streets of never-ending interest or to study the exteriors of the churches into which it was then too late to enter. One warm evening, when the heat had been well-nigh unbearable, we sought the river and rented a little boat in which to go a-voyaging. We carefully selected the cleanest among the number, which seemed dry and comfortable as well, and started happily in search of the so-called "floating gardens" or "hortillonages" beyond the city. The valley here is wide and very flat and the Somme in olden days lost itself in marshes and stagnant streamlets, which much later joined forces again and became once more a river of navigable size and importance. All the land through which it thus aimlessly loitered was virtually wasted and was besides a fertile breeding-ground for mosquitoes and other disease bearing things. A good many years ago this part was drained by the construction of narrow intersecting canals. The rich black mud dug from them had to go somewhere and was dumped upon the low-lying ground between, raising the level of it often a foot or more above the surrounding water. The thrifty inhabitants at once realized that here was the ideal site for the vegetable gardens needed for this great and growing city. The soil was rich, water was to be had for the effort of dipping it up, while only a primitive barge and a little poling were needed to float the produce to market. And so it proved to be. These rectangular or odd-shaped bits of land stretch for miles, each one a garden plot in which thrive all manner of vegetables, one succeeding the other as the season advances. J. T. poled us up and we were charmed by the beauty and interest of the trip. At first edging trees hung over the wider waterway on which we found ourselves, and back-door cottage gardens, their borders gay with old-fashioned flowers, came down to the stream's edge. Then the canals grew smaller, with the high, flat " jardins potagers " on either side, and people still working in them by the evening light. The water was clear and fast-running, the thick reedy grass so characteristic of small French rivers lying long and low in the current, with quantities of small fish similar to dace darting in and out. Across one high patch of artichokes we had a fascinating glimpse of the cathedral, a branch of the stiff decorative plants and their heavy pointed blossoms framing it on either side. So interested were we, so absorbed in all that was to be seen, that it was quite a while before we noticed that the slight moisture in the boat had increased so materially that it seemed wise to go ashore and empty it. We found this, however, not so easy. The steep banks of each garden made landing a most difficult performance and we went on and on in search of a better spot. Suddenly the water began to come in even faster and the deeper our craft settled, the more new leaks developed and poured in added streams until we were in danger of immediate submersion. I had lurid visions of the darting fish and of the slimy weeds winding themselves about my ankles, then a lower shore offered hope. I jumped to dry land with J. T. following me, and, as his foot left the seat to which he had taken final refuge, our worthy craft ignominiously sank! Luckily for us the water was very shallow, so we succeeded in pulling out our boat, emptying a good part of the canal from its

AMIENS
WATCHING THE PEOPLE BELOW
Size of the original etching, 4⅞ inches by 8⅛ inches

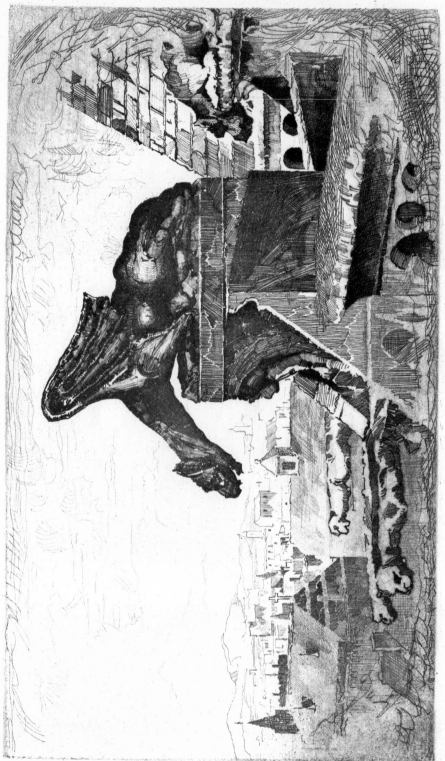

AMIENS
GUARDIANS OF THE SPIRE
Size of the original etching, 6¾ inches by 9⅞ inches

GUARDIANS OF THE SPIRE
Size of the original etching, 6¾ inches by 9⅞ inches

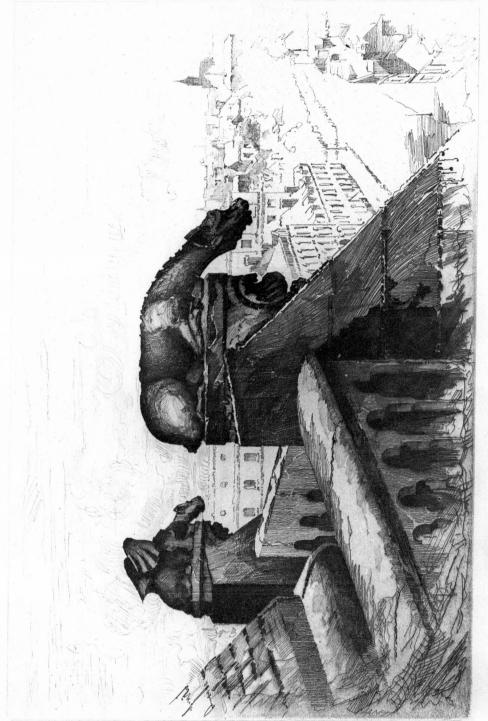

John Taylor Arms

capacious interior and launching it once more, damp but afloat. We decided then, and our guess proved correct, that it only leaked slightly at the bottom and that it took a considerable time for that little to accumulate sufficient weight to bring the boat low enough in the water for other and more serious leaks to manifest themselves. From then on the progress was positively arithmetical, until the final line of holes spouted water as from open taps. By keeping a watchful eye upon the situation we felt we would and could anticipate any further trouble, for we were distinctly anxious to avoid a second shipwreck in the wider, swifter, deeper waters of the Somme. The end of the floating gardens was in sight and a few minutes found us out upon the river, where all the town seemed to be enjoying its leisure according to taste; on the banks, older people sat and watched the passing show, children played and young couples walked with arms entwined in happy oblivion. On the stream, boys rowed races strenuously, older men progressed more slowly and lovers drifted with the current, two by two. The light was failing rapidly and the water broke into golden, dancing ripples. Through the trees we could see the cathedral, presiding with calm majestic grandeur over the city, a glorious silhouette against the glowing sky.

BEAUVAIS

TO make the perfect cathedral, tradition says one must take the portals of Rheims, the nave of Amiens, the towers of Chartres and the choir of Beauvais. The combination would be stupendous, naturally, and yet I doubt if the result would be the sum total of their separate and individual qualities; I think, rather, that each would lose something by its very juxtaposition with so much perfection. Our physical vision is limited and so too is our ability to absorb and appreciate beauty. Too much of anything goes beyond our receptive powers, as light rays which beat too fast upon the retina for the human eye to see and sound waves too high for the human ear to distinguish. The presence of an unfinished thing gives greater value to that which has been carried to completion and something a little less than perfection throws into even higher relief the perfect whole by very force of contrast. So Fujiyama, rising from its lowly plain, appears loftier, more mysterious, more unattainable than higher peaks which barely overtop their neighbours.

Beauvais, I am sure, is greater alone than it would be in such goodly company as this tradition has selected for it. It is more magnificent, more heart-touching as a fragment of the gigantic dream of Titan builders than it ever could have been had the original design been carried out. No one could feel that this soaring choir and these glorious transepts are a failure, yet in actual size they are only a part of the original plan and structurally they have proved too unsound to carry the immense weight destined for them. For all that, or partially because of it, this accomplished portion of a great conception is more inspiring, more truly beautiful than most completed churches. It stands pre-eminently for man's boundless aspiration, and, more than anything else, it makes me believe in perfection. The vision was there, only the limitations of human knowledge and the physical properties of stone and mortar kept it from fulfillment. But the dream was the thing, the ability to conceive a plan on such a scale, the daring courage to attempt it and the religious zeal to carry through such an undertaking. In the eyes of the builders they failed of their purpose, to us, who see what they accomplished, their so-called failure is the most magnificent and successful monument to man's inherent, undying belief in God.

BEAUVAIS
THE ROSE, BEAUVAIS
Size of the original etching, 12⅛ inches by 7¼ inches

John Taylor Arms 1925

As we approached Beauvais through undulating fields of ripening grain we were all eager for the first sight of town or cathedral. A turn of the road on a hillside finally rewarded us and we looked with shortened breath upon the picture presented to our view. The town sank into insignificance, all we could see was the immense structure which reared its rectangular mass high above its surroundings. From this distance it was not particularly ecclesiastical in appearance, we missed the usual length of nave and the height of tower or spire, but for sheer size it was overwhelming. We never lost that first impression. As we drew nearer, it appeared even bigger and when we stood and looked up to the northern transept set high on its base of fourteen broad steps, up to the glorious rose window framed between mighty turrets covered by fairylike sculptures, and still up to the pediment, its crisp angles and bold crockets silhouetted against the sky, we felt that we must be looking at some stupendous feat of nature rather than at a man-made monument.

Everywhere is this feeling of immensity. The apse, each stage so unbelievably high, lacks thereby some of the grace of the stepped-back effect which Le Mans has to such a marked degree but gains in a soaring quality of magnificent size. The interior is perhaps even more striking in this feeling. My first sensation on entering has always been one of awe and almost of physical fear. It does not seem possible that those slender, clustered piers can continue to support the weight of the vaulting, in itself so far away that it appears mysteriously dim in the vast distance. The atmosphere seems rarefied as on a mountain peak, breathing is a bit difficult and my head swims a little with the wonder and the sheer magnitude of it all. It takes time to grow accustomed to thinking on such a scale and one must go back again and yet again before one can begin really to see the wealth of detail and the purity of proportion of this most extraordinary and beautiful church.

There are evidences everywhere of the structural weaknesses which ended the dreams of town and clergy for the greatest building in the world. The soaring piers are not quite straight, a bulge here and an unplanned curve there reveal the disastrously heavy weight of the vaulting, while modern iron rods tie together arches spreading from the same cause. Over the crossing a wooden roof closes in the spot where once rose the lantern of Jean Vast, the pride of the city. The building of this and its failure symbolize the tragedy of the whole church and the end of a dream of divine beauty.

To raise money for this new project in 1535, Cardinal Odet de Chatillon granted indulgences to the faithful who, visiting the seven altars of the cathedral, left generous offerings there. He also permitted the consumption of milk and butter during Lent to those willing to pay for the privilege. Stone was commandeered at an arbitrary price rather to the dismay of the more conservative chapter, and later part of the treasure was sold to replenish the fund. So high was this spire, so slender and pierced by carving, that even during the building of it experts and laymen feared for its solidity. Committees met, learned men came from afar to pass on its safety. But finally, in 1569, the beautiful thing was complete and perfect, and the bishop of Beauvais, the priests, the canons and all the townspeople might boast to all and sundry that they had achieved a structural and artistic miracle. For four years their claim was justified, though they were troubled years for those in charge. There are constant records of this or that done to strengthen the substructure, of one expert having said so-and-so or another expert having recommended something else. By the middle of April 1573, finally convinced that drastic measures must be taken, the necessary workmen had been summoned by the dilatory chapter. But it was too late then, perhaps it would have been too late even at the very beginning. That delicate spire may have been meant to exist only as an exquisite memory, a burst bubble of incredible beauty. It was the thirtieth of April, Ascension Day, and the congregation and priests had just left the church to form in a procession, when, with a sound like thunder, the lantern fell. In a few moments its ethereal loveliness became an unrecognizable heap of shattered stone. The dazed people found themselves miraculously unharmed — only two priests at service in the older church were injured — but their pride lay in dusty ruins.

Several arches and columns had broken with the fall of the spire and the whole building seemed threatened with complete collapse. Ragged masses of stone hung precariously from the torn walls high overhead and the only safety lay in removing them before they fell of their own weight, bringing worse destruction with them. But no one would volunteer for the dangerous task; physical and possibly superstitious fear of the ill-omened building held them back. The situation became acute and finally it was decided to offer a condemned criminal his life if he would undertake the necessary work. He had nothing to lose and all to gain and the chance must have looked a golden one to him, yet with what human fears and misgivings must he have started on his dangerous labor. He succeeded, the menace was removed and life was his, to better or mar again. History, unfortunately, does not tell us the end of it.

And so ended the most aspiring, the most dramatic tale of Gothic building.

All the rest was an anticlimax of hiding the damage and preventing worse. We look up at the wooden roof which shows the outline but nothing more of that soaring spire. It is the scar of the wound to ecclesiastical ambition and stands as a memorial for all time to the religious fervor which could conceive of such a stupendous scheme but one which outstripped the physical strength of stone and mortar to complete it.

An incident happened in Beauvais which, slight enough in itself, was yet so typical of the fineness of type often found in the old provincial families that I feel it bears repeating. It was our first experience of the kind and it proved a very lovely foundation upon which we later built the sturdy edifice of our affection and admiration for the people of France.

As is our custom, we spent the first hours of our sojourn roaming about in search of the most appealing point of view. With the church always in mind, we walked up and down the radiating streets from which it could be seen completely or in part. Then, in order to be quite sure, we went farther off and circled the town for a possible distant view. But the first, though perhaps the most obvious choice, was also the most characteristic — a vista of a quiet street where all the lines of houses and walls led harmoniously to the great portal and delicate rose window of the south transept. From here we noticed less the unfinished quality of the whole and the blank west wall, while we kept the height, the justness of proportion and detail, and the exquisite grace which makes this one of the beauty spots of all times. So there in that quiet backwater of a street J. T. set up his stool and went to work while I strolled back from time to time to enthuse over some newly discovered bit of loveliness, or to laugh over some amusing episode. Often I found one or more persons standing quietly beside him, especially three, one a young man who lived in the pension before the great gates of which J. T. seemed to be more or less permanently established, who apologized each time he emerged from them and trusted that he was not disturbing Monsieur by passing. (Imagine feeling apologetic towards the person who was the intruder, after all!) The second was a workman, who when he came home at noon, was so much interested in the drawing and its creator that he could hardly tear himself away. He invited J. T. for luncheon, offered him wine and finally, in a last effort, pressed upon him some of his own tobacco, the strong rank perique which the French love and which J. T. smoked because courtesy demanded it but with woeful inner chokings. And the third was an old gentleman, gentle, polished of manner, soft of voice. He insisted on getting a chair for me, and as he came and went on business or on errands, he tarried each time for a little chat. Once, coming home from market with a basket on his arm and a long loaf of bread in his hand, he stopped for quite a time, and talked to me of America, of the war, of politics. A friend came by and joined us, the young man emerged from his pension gate and stopped also, still others paused to add their word or two as they walked or bicycled by us. It was a regular *conférence*. We talked of the condition of the franc, of their faith in the future recovery of the French financial position, and as the conversation grew exciting the old gentleman emphasized each point by tapping the ground with the staff of life which he carried. He told of the feeling in France when the news came that the first American soldiers had actually come. "We were tired," he said, "tired and discouraged. Then came the knowledge that your country, young, rich and with millions of men at her command, had sent fresh troops to bring hope as well as reinforcement to our army. We thanked God in the Cathedral and in our homes for you!" He spoke of the attacks from the air when the German planes tried again and again to reach the church, until the Pope sent a message saying that one more raid would mean that a detachment of picked French fliers would fly over to the Rhine and bomb their beloved cathedral at Cologne. "After that," he said, "there were no more attempts."

His wife came home from Mass, small, slender, with snow white hair and brown eyes — crystal clear until the mention of war brought a deepened look of horror to them. They had lost their sons during the long four years and had no child or grandchild to carry on their honored name nor to bring them companionship in their old age. They invited us in to see their home at the gates of which I sat. It was a beautiful and peaceful place. Built just after the cathedral, and of the superfluous stone, it had been inhabited by only two families before their own, the arms of which were carved on the massive staircase which led up from the inner courtyard. The rooms were spacious and beautifully proportioned, showing in their sculptured woodwork and their faded frescoes the vanished glories of a storied past. It was all very simple now, in spite of the grandeur of the setting and the beauty of the old furniture. It was easy to see that financial ease had gone with the war, as it had with many, many others.

They were so good to us. He arranged for us to see the great clock in the church, whose only rival is the one at Strasbourg, and which — according to our naturally prejudiced host — is neither as beautiful nor as unique as this. Thanks to him we visited it alone, free to ask questions and really see and

[26]

understand it a little more clearly. It was he also who arranged for my visit to the most interesting workrooms of the Gobelin tapestries, and in every possible way he looked out for our comfort and welfare. The last morning J. T. took an armful of flowers for the dear brown-eyed lady, as our only means of expressing our appreciation, and that evening as the last pencil was packed away and we were about to knock on that hospitable door to say our good-byes, it swung wide as if by magic and there they stood to welcome us and wish us bon voyage. He picked a flower for me and presented it with his courteous bow of other days and the remark that it was the flower of France for an American lady. When I turned to her, she held out both hands to me and said, "I love your flowers and I am enjoying them to-day — but to-morrow, as you start on your journey, I am taking them to the Cathedral where I shall lay them on the altar of Our Lady, as an offering for the success of your trip and for the health and safety of your children."

Years later our wandering road led us back to Beauvais. Once more we knocked at the great oak door which had opened to us so graciously before. This time the little old gentleman stood there alone. His wife had made her last journey to her dearly loved cathedral and he was living on yet a little while, in memories.

BAYEUX

NOTRE DAME of Bayeux, though a distinct composite of styles, yet gives the impression of unusual unity and harmony. The greater part of it is Norman Gothic, the west towers are Romanesque and the high lantern over the crossing is largely Renaissance, but this mixture only goes to prove that the beauties of different types and periods may live together in perfect harmony, may in fact act as complementary foils and so increase the charm, one of the other. In this magnificent cathedral one feels this especially, there is a fundamental sweep of according lines which the variety of detail only serves to accentuate.

The first recorded history of its building dates from the eleventh century, though little of the original edifice remains. The western towers are part of this oldest construction. They are almost identical and very harmonious, varying just enough to add charm and richness. The lower stories are pierced by narrow round-arched windows and have columns with simple capitals, and the pediments of the porch are lightened by Gothic penetrations of cusped circles. Above all one feels that strength and durability so characteristic of Norman architecture, and with it all a certain warmth and lavishness of detail which adds a graciousness and a charm to a style erring sometimes on the side of too much austerity.

The interior is in my opinion the finest part. When I first saw it, I sat alone long hours in the nave, letting the color of its stone and the harmony of its lines sink into my mind and heart. I visited it later with the Younger Generation, avid to see every nook and corner, every bit of the treasure, every sculptured capital; and I saw it at the time of the Feast of the Assumption, full of people and light and color, with all the ceremony of a procession; and each time, under every condition, I found it a truly religious, truly churchly church.

The arches of the nave are Romanesque and not only is the decoration of each one different, but the lightly chiseled patterns which cover the spandrels and the primitive — almost grotesque — sculptures in the pedentives, are absolutely dissimilar. Above the round arches runs a delicate Gothic triforium, and still above that are large clerestory windows, each pair separated by columns quite free of the walls. The transepts are a mass of detail strongly Flam-

BAYEUX
THE CATHEDRAL OF NOTRE DAME
Size of the original pencil drawing, 17 inches by 9⅜ inches

John Douglas Hunt

boyant in character, with blind arches of frail tracery, and the columns behind the choir are fluted, with leafy capitals. Yet in spite of this apparent mixture of styles, it is one of those interiors where one feels rhythm and homogeneity.

We were in Bayeux one August for the celebration of the Feast of the Assumption. The great gilt statue of the Virgin which we had already seen in the Chapter Room, was to be carried in solemn procession to the church of St. Martin at the other end of town, and back again. There was a solemn service first. The great central doors stood wide open and through them we could see the shifting play of light and color, while the music came to us in broken snatches. It was beautiful and mysterious, we felt the age-old reverence, the eternal faith. Then a heterogeneous mass of people streamed out and stood about in ragged groups while a bustling beadle endeavored to organize the procession, and then the illusion went as suddenly as a snuffed-out candle. I think I never saw such dirty boys. Their red suits were spotty and greasy, from under the uneven hems shabby boots with broken laces protruded stubbily, and wrinkled hose completed the picture. Their coarse cotton cottas were of that indescribable grayish hue which only soiled white can be, and their hands were beyond description. It seemed so disrespectful, somehow; cleanliness at least is possible, however poor the modern church may be. In striking contrast were the priests; their lace was rich and beautifully laundered and they wore squirrel or ermine stoles, not for the warmth but as insignia of office. The procession gradually got under way. The sacred statue went first, carried jerkily on unaccustomed shoulders, then came the priests chanting in deep sonorous tones the ever repeated Ave Maria, while the following crowd responded with Ora Pro Nobis.

They were a motley lot, small boys in sailor suits and quantities of little girls in all tones and shades of blue. These were the children who, vowed to the Madonna at birth, must wear only her color and white for the first seven years of their lives. There were nuns, many so young that one realizes that a religious life is not only the calling but it is as well the only vocation for many of the thousands of women who cannot marry in this land where the number of men is greatly inferior and where a dowry is a necessity. After these came the women who belonged to the great society known as the Association of the Children of Mary, a powerful organization.

The people formed in two columns, each line walking in the gutter at the extreme edge of the street, and they made an interesting study of assorted types and characters. Even the way they walked revealed their outlook on life : some hurried awkwardly, others marched with conscious slowness, some greeted friends on the pavement with a cheerful word or smile, others kept their eyes stonily before them. One woman particularly impressed me. She was very large and had compressed her ample figure into a close-fitting dress of bright green jersey. Above her broad, complacent face rose the peasant coif of this section, a white cap on a snug black velvet band with a stiffly starched bowknot behind. She rolled along, her deep-chested responses clear and resonant, satisfied with herself, at peace with the world.

Later, the procession came back along the same way and filed into the cathedral for the final service. We went in also, and stood on the elevated platform which is just inside the entrance. From it five steps lead down into the body of the church, so that from here we had an uninterrupted view of the interior and recaptured once more the mystery and the feeling of religious meaning. Standing with our backs against the central pillar of the great carved doors, we looked down on the congregation assembled in the body of the church below us, then up that long magnificent nave in which variety and unity are so perfectly blended, to the choir where above massed flowers, white for the Virgin's purity, candles burned steadily. Three apsidal windows containing almost the only painted glass in the building were visible from where we stood ; the center one of golden tone was so perfectly in alignment that it needed no surveyor's instruments to know that here was an apse which did not incline to the north. The late sunlight touched the transept wall with pale radiance and the nave gleamed with strange tones filtered through the grisaille glass of the clerestory, a color neither yellow nor green but luminously both. The organ pealed, voices chanted as a priest intoned in high-pitched cadences, and it was easy to let a few centuries slip from one's shoulders and be back in the days of Bayeux' first and greatest glory.

The eleventh century saw the completion of the cathedral and was enriched by the lives of a family whose deeds and whose characters changed the whole history of the western world. Most famous was William, who with a bravado born of bitterness, signed his name the Bastard until his successful campaign in England gave him the right to the well-earned title of Conqueror. The stories of him are legion, tales of his wisdom, his justice, his rages, even of his strange wooing. Angered by Mathilda's refusal to marry him, he waylaid her as she left church, knocked her down, rolled her in the mud, and threw stones at her, with the result that the duly impressed young lady went home with

John Taylor Arms 1928

aching bones and throbbing bruises and announced to her father that her husband was to be William or nobody.

Without her steadying influence his reign could never have been as great as it was, although it would have undoubtedly been a very fine one. Through all the accounts, history or legend, one feels her personality like a strong silken strand, which, though lustrous and soft and beautiful, yet holds fast when stronger materials fray and break. She was a devoted wife and mother, a diplomat and a true queen. Appointed regent in William's absence, she governed with good common sense tempered by loving understanding of her people. When he returned she slipped back gladly into second place, taking her part in affairs of state but supervising her household as well, planning the meals with her chief steward and keeping the peace between her forceful, intolerant husband and their headstrong elder son. The only record of a rift in the perfect marital happiness of this extraordinary pair is the one where William, coming in upon Mathilda unexpectedly, found her gathering money to send to the banished boy who was plotting and planning against his father and his duchy. He taxed her with disloyalty but her reply was that of all true mothers. Whatever he was, whatever he did, he was her son, her first born, and her heart and her help were his for the asking. There was a tempestuous scene and after that no mention of continued financial aid, though Mathilda interceded between them again and again and succeeded several times in bringing about temporary reconciliations.

They had much sorrow from their children. History does not record how many of these there were — ten perhaps. Most of those we know were tragic figures — this older son who inherited his father's weaknesses but not his virtues, two others who were killed while hunting — William's favorite pastime, which he indulged to a fault — William Rufus, tyrannical and brutal king of England, and Elgiva, whose story reads like an idyll of Tennyson. This daughter was betrothed to Harold when, in the labyrinth of plots and counter-plots, hidden motives and vaulting ambitions, he promised William his aid in securing him the English throne. When he himself ascended that throne on Edward's death, he broke faith with the daughter as well as the father and married one of his own countrywomen. Elgiva mourned his defection and when the news reached her of his tragic death, her grief was inconsolable. But she came of noble blood, to whom the call of duty is above personal feelings. She was an asset, a possible link to hold Normandy close to some other power. William obtained her consent to marry the king of Galicia. A heartbroken bride, she sailed away with her chests of magnificent clothes and coffers of rich jewels, and with a prayer on her lips that she might die before she reached her destination. Her wish was granted. Before the voyage was over her spirit had slipped away, her ship was turned about and came back sorrowfully, bringing only the tired body of an obedient child for burial in the choir of the Cathedral of Bayeux.

I lost a dearly-loved illusion when I discovered that the famous tapestry of Queen Mathilda is neither a tapestry nor a work done by her or under her direction. I did not mind finding it an embroidery, but I sadly regretted losing the charming picture of a gracious and beautiful queen sitting among her ladies, talking of the exploits of husbands or fathers or brothers, planning each woven picture, setting the endless stitches whose verve and dramatic feeling have been a marvel for years. To Odo, half-brother of William, seems to belong the credit for the conception of this piece of work, and praise for the workmanship belongs to English labor.

This Odo was the son of William's mother after her marriage to Count Herlwen. He possessed many of his brother's qualities of leadership but not his personal virtues. Accounts differ; some chronicle him as a wise administrator, fair and farseeing, others as an unjust tyrant. His character seems to have been pretty thoroughly condemned even in that era of casual morals but I wonder if that has not been accentuated by a natural bias in favor of the brother in power. Odo was twelve, or some say seventeen, when William made him Bishop of Bayeux, a rank piece of family preferment to which our own much criticized age of political graft would not dream of stooping. He took this clever younger brother with him on his campaigns. His valor and his military strategy were never questioned yet there seems to have been a constant state of friction between the two. Jealousy, perhaps, who knows? William was illiterate and illegitimate, Odo was well read, polished and with no stain upon his parentage. Also they were both overweeningly ambitious and the elder was too keen a man not to have recognized, and possibly feared, the latent power in the younger.

Sorcerers in Rome predicted that on Gregory's death the pope to succeed him would be named Odo. That was enough for the Normandy prelate. He hired a Roman palace and ordered sumptuous furnishings, he sent fabulous gifts to people high in church power and he gathered knights and followers about him for the journey to Italy. William heard, and hurrying to England reached him as he was about to embark. He ordered his arrest but no one dared touch him, so he carried it through himself. Odo claimed exemption on the ground that only a pope could arrest a bishop, but William replied that he was not interested in the ecclesiastical side, he was a king arresting a treacherous earl.

Nothing succeeds like success, an old adage but a true one. If Odo had carried through his plan, had reached Rome and by force of his personality, his statesmanship and the immense value of the psychological moment, had managed to have himself made pope, how would history speak of him? As a great leader I am sure. The man with a vision who, willing to leave the beaten path of safety, yet fails, is branded a blind fool by public opinion but if the weight of a straw turns the scales in his favor, then the world acclaims him great. There is no difference in the man himself, only the accident of success.

So Odo, powerful though he was, only reached the lesser heights. Yet his pride, his extravagance, his love of beauty had one constructive result. He ordered the tapestry, probably for use in the cathedral at its consecration in 1077 when William, Mathilda, Robert, William Rufus and all the brilliant courtiers were present. They are all gone, but their memory is vivid and alive partly because of themselves, partly because of their deeds and partly because they live perennially in that length of gaily embroidered grayish linen.

COUTANCES

SITUATED on a steep hill to which the wind brings a stimulating burden of salt air fresh from the ocean near at hand, the town of Coutances seems to have drawn itself up into a remote seclusion. The main highway circles it near the base of the eminence on which it is built, avoiding the mounting road which leads up past the church of St. Pierre to the cathedral on the summit. The houses are shuttered, the streets empty, everything dreams under the guardianship of so much beauty.

We arrived here one late afternoon after a drive along the sea, where the villages of bleak stone houses betrayed the severity of winter, yet which showed us a gracious mood of sun-warmed sands and tumbling blue water, deeply purple where the cloud shadows fell. Whichever road we took from the plain brought us around the town instead of up into it. Each time we thought that finally we were upon the right one, only to find ourselves shortly on the other side of the hill with the church behind, instead of before us. However, so lovely was each view from no matter what side, that our decision to tarry for a few days was soon reached, and feeling that we might have better success if we made a fresh beginning, we started in search of a hotel. Our heretofore trusty guidebook recommended one which rejoiced in the good old name of "Les Trois Rois," but omitted all mention of its street. With unerring fatality the first man of whom we inquired the way was deaf but anxious to help us out. He limped hastily towards us, with an eager hand cupped behind his better ear. Now I know no letter more difficult for an Anglo-Saxon to pronounce than the French "r"; followed by an "oi" it is even worse and when in addition one has the mental hazard of ears which will find one's best none too good, it becomes an almost insuperable obstacle. J. T. propounded the necessary question, but with no success; he asked again and yet again, with the "r" growing flatter and flatter and the hopeful listening face more blank and puzzled at each repetition. When the dreaded words had lost all semblance of their original pronunciation, we gave up in despair and betook ourselves to the only other hotel in town, with a feeling of mortification only allayed by the discovery that "Les Trois Rois" had ceased to exist some five years earlier.

We soon learned the roads which would take us to our desired goal. One,

COUTANCES 1926.

John Taylor Arms 1927

a broad curve encircling the central part of town and swinging around at the summit, brought us on to the wide "place" which opens out before the cathedral. The other, rising steeply up between crowding lines of houses, reached the same point from the other side. It was from here that J. T. elected to make his drawing, for, though the cathedral was only visible in part, the church of St. Pierre could also be seen and the two served as beautiful foils, one for the other. This latter building is a gorgeous medley of Gothic and Renaissance architecture. The western tower is positively gay in its treatment — the square base, well covered by delicate ornament, transforms itself into an octagonal upper story, which becomes in turn a small high dome, almost Moorish in shape. The lantern over the crossing is massive and highly decorated, in fact the whole exterior with its quantity of sculptured detail is in curious contrast to the handling of the interior. Here the nave is short and rather flat, with heavy columns. Everything is built for strength, and ornamentation has been reduced to a minimum. The one lighter bit is a really lovely and graceful balustrade around the choir wall.

The Cathedral of Notre Dame is such an uncompromisingly pure example of the Norman style that only the great beauty and perfect harmony of its proportions keep it from being coldly severe. Built in the thirteenth century, with the exception of a few chapels added later, it has all the unity of design and singleness of vision which only comparative speed of construction can give. Different needs develop, thought changes and religious fervor waxes and wanes as the years slip by and, if building is going on, these shifting tides in the life about it must be reflected in the physical structure of the church. One century may take away, or one may add, but each leaves an indelible imprint of itself in the stones and mortar of the construction and writes a vivid history by these means.

As the always moving waters change the face of things, making new land here, or wearing away a coast line there, so — and with no more apparent reason — does the wave of national importance engulf a place, or receding, leave it stranded in unwonted peace. From Roman days the town of Coutances played a prominent rôle in the history of Normandy. A strategic point on its high hill, it dominated the surrounding countryside, and wide was the field of its influence. Now it is remote and rather isolated. The main arteries of travel pass to the south of it and only the fame of its cathedral serves to bring back a little life and animation to its streets. But even at that, the hurried traveler merely pauses, Coutances is only a detour to the omnivorous sight-seer. Yet if one can spare a few days the reward is rich. I know no lovelier example of its type than this Cathedral of Notre Dame — well named in spite of its size and strength, for its preëminent quality is a virginal purity.

The exterior is severely plain and detail has been almost completely suppressed. Only the sculptured gallery, high on the face of the façade, relieves the uncompromising verticality of the straight upward lines, while simple spire-like turrets crown the buttresses around the high, plain apse.

The interior is a little more elaborate, though there is a unity of form which only a slight variety in detail, such as the delicate sculptured rosettes in the spandrels, serves to soften. The lateral chapels have a feature which is so lovely in St. Nazaire at Carcassonne. Instead of solid walls dividing one from the other, here are open Gothic arches of lacelike tracery. This makes almost a five-aisled nave, increasing the sense of width and airy lightness.

On our last day in Coutances I was waiting in the car for J. T. to rejoin me with one more completed drawing in his knapsack. The great façade of the cathedral was in front of me and I sat lost in its beauty. As I gazed at the lofty spires, identical in size and only varied in treatment, I had the strange illusion which comes from looking up suddenly at a great height, the sensation that the building was moving against the sky, tipping towards me with a sickening swing. I had one flashing thought that, after all, it would be a unique death to go in the midst of crashing loveliness, then my sense of balance reasserted itself and I realized that the soaring towers remained as upright, as surely poised as they had stood through the centuries, and as the centuries to come may still hope to find them.

HONFLEUR

IN spite of the swarming tourist and in spite of the ubiquitous artist, Honfleur is still unspoiled. We had had a long drive along that seashore where money is as plentiful as the grains of sand, where hideous stucco villas shriek the lack of good taste among the French people who can still afford to build, where Normandy farmhouses are tricked up with gay umbrellas and scarlet geraniums into places where one is invited to partake of one's "five o'clock," and where striped tents vie with brilliant summer costumes in an effort to make the eternal sands bloom like a flower-garden. After this worldly world, with nature masquerading in artificial and exotic costumes, we wound a tortuous, precipitous way down the narrow streets of Honfleur, straight into the heart of a mediaeval town. Much is new, of course, but with its ancient houses, half-timbered, bricked or slated, its high pitched roofs with crowning dormers, its quays about which most of the commerce and social life of the inhabitants center, and with its ancient church, so expressive of the craft as well as the spirit of its builders, it is a vivid and impressive bit of a long ago time and an almost extinct type of living.

Built at the mouth of the Seine, at the spot where that meandering river, having serpentined a curving course through the historic plains of Normandy, finally reaches the sea through a wide shallow bay, Honfleur is almost equally divided into water and dry land. Its new port where water is held at will by gates, its tidal basins where the short, fat fishing schooners lie on their sides on muddy banks long hours every day until the incoming tide floats them back to normal uprightness, and its coast-line, part bay, part sea, make it a safe harbor. Poor little town, it was a strategic point in olden times and everyone either wanted it or trampled on it in passing. It seems to have been a veritable battle-ground until the fifteenth century, when comparative peace descended on it and public interest and military needs turned in a different direction. It became a great port then and traded in commodities of all varieties, including slaves. The interesting museum shows samples of the goods which the wealthy Rouen merchants traded for these unhappy people who were brought here in Honfleur boats, manned by her sailors, and who exchanged their hot land for this exposed coast where the sunshine is more than overpowered by the fine

[37]

steady rain which gives this section the name of "La Verte Normandie." They were bartered, not sold, so many meters of material were worth one negro. It seems doubly tragic; at least a human life should have a golden value. Pirates plied their trade from here and in 1608 Samuel Champlain, native of Honfleur, sailed away from his home town to found the city of Quebec.

The center of the town — both as far as the old, quaint streets are concerned and in the affections of the inhabitants — is the church of Ste. Cathérine, unique in its construction and one of the most sincere and direct of religious expressions. The belfry, separated from it by a small "place," is the more interesting to the passer-by, and the one to which the artist turns as a needle to the pole. One sees them all about on camp stools like overgrown mushrooms, reproducing it in oil, in water-color or in black and white. The old bells which clang so lustily that the flag-pole projecting from the side of its ancient steeple rocks as a ship at sea, must laugh slyly at the ever-changing, ever-similar, earnest faces which peer up at them or squint anxiously over some error in perspective. As a matter of fact there is no correct perspective in the whole building; no two lines are parallel, not an angle is true. The wider base is the home of the bell-ringer, and beautifully is he housed, if not with modern comfort and improvements. His front door is of massive wood and above it is a bit of delicate sculpture, his walls are half-timber and plaster, as are those of many of his neighbours, and in his irregular windows gay geraniums bloom. His high-pitched, lichened roof helps to support the lower part of the tower, and massive struts, slate-covered, complete the same structural function, acting as primitive flying buttresses between the roof and upper walls. Above them is the belfry proper, with its sharply curving spire terminating in a long, slender point. Why the tower and the church are apart remains a mystery. I could find no evidence of an earlier building of which the bell-ringer's lodge might be a fragment, yet it seems difficult to believe that it was originally built at such a distance. It is more picturesque as it is; the two, being separated, better frame the little "place" with its scenes of gaiety or of commerce, for here the markets are held, with stalls of meat or vegetables or brilliant fruit and with crowds of bargaining women. The men play a very insignificant part in the town. Their stronghold is the water-front, in the boats moored until next high water, or sitting in a conversational row upon the coping of the quays for hours on end, settling the affairs of the world to their complete satisfaction. The women reign in the market and haggle thriftily over golden melons, or long green pears, or tins of sweet crackers. On one side the belfry lifts a mis-

HONFLEUR
BELFRY OF THE CHURCH OF STE. CATHÉRINE
Size of the original pencil drawing, 13¾ inches by 7½ inches

John Taylor Arms 1928

chievous eyebrow, on the other the church smiles tranquilly at the doings of her children.

Ste. Cathérine was built in the middle of the fifteenth century to replace an older church, though not, it seems, on the exact site. The old streets approach it from all directions, and though it faces west in the conventional way its surroundings are so lacking in unity that it appears rather to have been set down casually, just anywhere. Its main façade is at an angle with the open "place" before it and the apse is best seen from such a point that one does not quite realize what the shape of it really is until one sees it from within. And this rather unsophisticated quality is very characteristic of the whole building. It was built by a simple people to fulfill a religious practical need, and so thoroughly does it express this spirit that it stands as one of the most completely unaffected and spontaneous churches in existence.

The inhabitants of Honfleur were, and still are, a seafaring race. Pirates ravaged their shores and burned their houses, and so it is no wonder that a marauding ship or two went forth adventuring in retaliation from this town so harried by invasion. Later, commerce by water became their chief means of livelihood, and shipbuilding went on at a lively rate. It is said that they provided William the Conqueror with eleven ships for his English expedition. So it was only natural that when they came to build their church it should be done in a style to which they were accustomed, with the materials of their daily use and by the builders in their midst. These latter were the shipwrights, the master-carpenters who designed and constructed boats to which so many of their townsmen daily entrusted their lives. With these as models, with the seasoned oak which was at hand and with their simple tools, they set themselves to the task of church-building.

Originally Ste. Cathérine had one nave terminating in a single, simple chapel, and two low aisles with lean-to roofs; later it was widened, making it as it stands to-day, with a nave of twin aisles and lower ones beyond, whose walls are of half-timber and plaster. The roof is supported by massive wooden piers instead of the usual columns. They are square and roughhewn, and under the brackets which help to support the side roofs are little carved figures, as the only decoration. Windows of plain glass rise above the height of the side aisles, forming a simple clerestory, and the vaulting is most curious and interesting. In curve and proportion and type, it is a perfect inverted keel of a ship. The northern nave is the original one and has the more beautiful line, that subtle reverse curve which only the hull of a boat ever has. In the roofing of the lower portions a fragment of the first vaulting is visible, uneven bits of wood — some with paint still clinging to them — fitted together to form a rude inner sheathing. We found the shape of these pieces puzzlingly characteristic, and they quite worried us until we realized that they must have been old barrel staves, cut and joined together. Across the organ-loft runs a most extraordinary band of wooden panels. They are Renaissance carvings of pagan subjects in light relief against a background of delicate arches, their depth cleverly suggested by subtle lines of perspective — Pan of the cloven hoof, Apollo with his lute and many other friends of mythological story. I could find no accurate information as to their origin, to me they suggested chest-fronts, set side by side, but why they should have been placed in that particular church, or, for that matter, in any church at all, I do not know. Perhaps for the musical instruments depicted in each panel.

Most of the windows are clear, with a few simple stained ones in the twin apses. Low openings at this end are leaded with circles of greenish glass, which either actually are deadlights or are meant to simulate those opaque rounds used on sailing ships to mitigate the gloom below decks.

In 1820 the decadent taste of an age which mistook standardization for unity and which saw no beauty in anything which varied from the safe lines of accepted models, endeavored to make an up-to-date building of this church of the people, one which would be like countless others. They plastered the wooden pillars and made round columns of them with conventional capitals, they covered the keel-vaulting with a modern ceiling and they removed the lean-to porch on the western end to make a massive Neo-Greek front, complete even to the lintel and pediment! Fortunately they destroyed little, and a more discerning generation has removed the hideous incongruities and has uncovered the original and significant beauty. Even the porch, the last thing to be restored, is being rebuilt now according to the old design, the speed of it depending on the state of the hopeful alms-box inside the door, which pleads for the necessary funds. Soon Ste. Cathérine will be herself again and her simple, faithful builders may once more sleep untroubled in their graves.

Near Honfleur is a little town called Pont l'Évêque. It is on the highroad, with many points of social, industrial or architectural interest nearby. This fact makes it slightly known to the hurried passer-by, yet rarely more than slightly because of his anxiety to get on to the next place. Its church of St. Michel is not a great monument, but the west façade is a striking example of the plain Norman style, unmodified, unchanged for many years. We, our-

PONT L'ÉVÊQUE
CHURCH OF ST. MICHEL
Size of the original etching, 9¼ inches by 5 inches

PONT L'ÉVÊQUE
CHURCH OF ST. MICHEL
Size of the original etching, 9¼ inches by 5 inches

Église St. Michel, Pont l'Evêque

John Taylor Arms 1917

selves, were about to pass it by when a fortunate vista up a brief street revealed a square, truncated tower curiously roofed. Later we came back to draw, and later still came from Honfleur to see it once again.

The keynote of the church is a massive solidity. It was built for use by a sturdy people accustomed to war and hard living. The exterior has been modified by Flamboyant motives, but they cannot conceal the rugged structural strength of the building. There is no western door, nor evidence that there ever was one, though its absence only serves to accentuate the weight and severity of that untouched façade. Above it is the abortive tower, supported by stepped-back buttresses and topped by a high-pitched temporary roof of slate. One wonders at the piety which could build so far and then leave it incomplete through years and centuries.

The interior has the same feeling. There is a narthex with low vaulting under the west tower; the first piers of the nave are tremendous, then come smaller ones, round and sturdy, with no capitals; the groining begins in the shafts and rises up into the vaulting much as one sees it in the Gros Piliers at Mont Saint Michel. The aisles are low, with too heavy vaulting and deep, elaborate, weighty keys in which grouped animals, children with uplifted arms, and grotesques succeed each other with a feeling of strained effort after variety. The great piers of the crossing are so large that spiral staircases are built comfortably within them. Everything is massive, rather low and heavy, a quality which the exterior carries off with greater dignity than the interior. This church is as typical of its builders as the wooden one of Ste. Cathérine, only here the highroad had brought them knowledge of the growth of Gothic buildings and they used and adapted the style to their own needs and their own forceful characters.

There was a fête for the war wounded on our one Sunday in Honfleur. The night before a destroyer had braved the tidal harbor and come up right into the heart of the city to honor the occasion; there had been an excellent band concert in a little square under gay, flickering lanterns as many colored as Joseph's proverbial coat; and in the morning cannon crackers had roused us from untroubled slumbers at a quite unearthly hour. The little town fairly seethed with martial music and moving crowds, culminating in the high memorial Mass at eleven o'clock. Never having been able to resist a drum, I found myself in the open "place" before the church at the moment when the parade arrived. It was not a great one, perhaps, but so sincere, so absolutely spontaneous that I watched with a troublesome lump in my throat. First came a little group of gendarmes and pompiers, then a band of boys of all ages, in white with broad blue ribbons about their waists and white berets at a coquettish angle on their heads. After them came the veterans, most of them the war wounded whose special day this was, more tragic than usual as they limped to the spirited music with an effort at military time or swung an empty sleeve as they marched along. A shabby business suit, shiny from too much pressing, which showed a brave array of medals upon its worn lapel, struck me as being a more inspiring sight than even greater decorations on the uniformed chest of a regular soldier. I looked at the ten boys who represented the navy, in their sea-going sailor suits and white tams with gay red pom-poms, and at the army band of lads in horizon blue who brought up the rear of the procession, and I thought of the thoughtless youngsters who, during the first days of the war, had gone so gaily forth from their last Mass in this their religious home. Some of them never came back, others returned as the living dead who were wheeled along in chairs, or marched mutilated, with undying spirit. Such a very few returned unharmed.

Most of the procession straggled in through the western door, while those of greater importance, preceded by flags, walked with a little more effort at formation through the southern one. I followed the former as inconspicuously as possible and took my stand against the farthest wall under the organ-loft. The church was filled to capacity and every seat and bench was long since taken. The aisles were crowded with standing people of all sorts and conditions, and, so far as I could see, I was the only stranger there. Near me stood a chauffeur in his smart white linen coat, blue-collared; a service-ribbon showed in the buttonhole under his livery. Beyond him there was a staid, black-gowned, black-hatted "vieille fille" of Normandy, whom Balzac has made such a familiar figure, and beside me stood a young soldier and an older man who carried himself with the upstanding angularity of a veteran. Across his chest the gold watch chain and black eyeglass ribbon of his present-day costume competed with a decoration and two medals. From where I stood I could see the altar indistinctly over the sea of moving heads between. There was the sheen of silken banners, bright with the pure, clear colors of France, and the light of many candles, some of them very near the floor. There was the ceaseless shuffle of restless feet, over which carried only an occasional staccato remark from the priest; organ music alternated with that of the youthful band, and old hymns were sung instead of the usual rather monotonous chant. The sun, streaming through the uncolored windows, made long shafts of golden light in the dust-filled air. At noon, with the last organ peals of the recessional, the blare of marching instruments and the clanging bells of the near-by belfry vieing with one another in joyful clamor, the congregation and the spectators went their separate ways. I slipped into the church to see at closer range the decoration of banked flowers and massed flags, and the reason for the low-placed candles before the altar. I had thought myself alone in the building, which seemed unusually deserted in contrast to the recent scene of animation which it had housed, but as I came into the aisle I realized my mistake. In the open space before the sanctuary loving and remembering hands had built two graves of grass and flowers. Candles burned on either side and at the head of each grave was a little cross. On one lay the gray-blue coat and trench-helmet of a soldier, on the other the dark blue jacket and gay red pom-pommed cap of a sailor. Kneeling before them was the solitary black-gowned figure of a woman.

CAUDEBEC–EN–CAUX

THIS section of France is so rich in historical and architectural treasures that the trouble is not to find the perfect subject, but rather to decide on only one out of the great mass of possible material. There is Jumièges, which haunts one's memory with its ruined beauty about which nature has flung a healing, concealing veil of brilliant green. There is St. Wandrille, where ghosts walk and where the spirit of Maeterlinck must live again the hours of creative thought spent in these hallowed precincts. The parish church nearby is very old and is crowded with life-size statues of saints. This is a pilgrimage church where people come year by year to ask some boon. They tie a long white tape to the image of the saint in whom they have most confidence, until some have become an indistinguishable mass of graying ribbons, while others look forlorn with perhaps only one token or two hung from a plaster finger. There is a little church whose name I have forgotten, built on the narrow ledge of a cliff. We saw it above us as we passed one day. We stopped, scrambled up a steep and uninviting bank and were ushered into a tiny chapel built on and into the living rock. The floor is of the natural stone, roughly smoothed and with the deeper crevasses filled in to make more secure footing. Half of the primitive vaulting is the overhanging rock of the hill, only the outer part is man-built. This is truly a church far from the unstable house of the parable built upon the sands, yet in spite of the centuries of its life one wonders how soon a hard winter of snow and ice-filled cracks will come and push forward that inner wall, tumbling the whole building to destruction.

Then there is Caudebec-en-Caux, no more beautiful perhaps than many others but with a gay, appealing personality and a church tower of tempting delicacy. So Caudebec claimed us for a little while.

It is the busiest place for its size, there seems to be something happening on land or sea at every hour of the day and night. Our first introduction to it was characteristic. Coming around a curve of the road, we found ourselves without any warning in the midst of a herd of animals. They were neither the calm, contemplative cows nor the placid, patient oxen of this section, but large, young and lively bulls. The car was small and open. Charging among them

John Taylor Arms. Aug 26. 1926.

seemed hardly the indicated course, yet sitting still was difficult also as they filed slowly by with an occasional warning pass at us with a pair of sharp and curly horns. No one else seemed to notice them, everyone was busy about his or her affairs.

The Seine here is wide and hurries between its low green banks as if anxious to reach the sea only thirty-five miles away. At this spot the "mascaret" is best seen. At the time of the equinox, when the tides are at their highest, the water rushes up with irresistible force while the current only checks and angers it into boiling, tempestuous waves but does not seriously impede its progress. They tell tales of the strange roaring noise of its advance, of spray thrown incredible distances into the air and of damage done along the banks. There are records of farms swept completely away, of an island opposite Caudebec which had disappeared when the tide ebbed and of boats — caught in the fury — overturned or sunk.

Since time immemorial the river has been the highway for Caudebec and all the towns which are built upon its banks, and even now, with trains and roads linking them together, still the river holds its own. Boats work a dogged, difficult way up against the current, taking advantage of an incoming tide for greater speed, but when they make the return journey then it is a very different matter. They leave Paris or Rouen, or whatever port it may be, planning to reach here when tide and current coincide, and their speed is quite remarkable. I never tired of watching the ever-similar yet ever-changing procession of them. When I saw one boat coming down the stream I knew that many others were close behind it. They came one by one, slipping along with no visible effort, yet so fast that the water cut by their passing made a continuous sound like that of a gentle surf. There were heavy-laden barges taking coal to England, a smart yacht or two with only enough white sails set to give steerage way, river steamers and larger boats carrying passengers to more distant ports. One would appear, come abreast of me with a rushing sound of water and vanish to the right as another appeared from the left, and another, and another until it seemed as if all the boats in France must be leaving the country that day. But finally they were all gone and the river was left to stumpy fishing boats and to the tiny ferry which plied an industrious trade from shore to shore, carrying people and bicycles, a horse or two or one automobile, according to its limited capacity. Sunday always saw a waiting line of cars on either bank.

The quays were almost as fascinating. Men fished from them endlessly, motors passed or stopped, dogs brought old feuds to a snarling climax, slow ox carts ground on their protesting way, char-à-bancs poured forth crowds of passengers, and busses, brave with white ribbons, brought wedding-parties who strolled about in the glory of their new finery.

Behind the quays lies the town which, in spite of its thriving, busy modern life, is ancient beyond belief. The charter for the markets, still held here on Saturdays, goes back in an unbroken line to the twelfth century. The waters of a little tributary of the Seine have been canalized and they hurry along with a cool, rushing sound past the houses or under the streets, checked here and there in their onward sweep to provide power for some small factory. Old houses lean across the narrow sidewalks and in more than one place one can stand in the center of the street with one's hands resting easily against the walls on either side.

In the center of a cobweb of little winding ways is the church of Notre Dame, an exquisite example of the Flamboyant Gothic style. The first impression — and the last — is one of joyous, lacelike delicacy. The façade has a triple porch similar to that of St. Maclou with its five portals, and is a marvel of minute detail. Even the spaces between the arches of the doors are a mass of sculpture, of which one unusual feature is the use of a small spire terminating in a tiny figure. Into each one of these has been put as much apparent thought and certainly as many motives as appear in the average church steeple.

A curious and incongruous gallery of large caryatids and the new white stone of recent restoration mar the upper portion of the façade. Around the roof runs a balustrade composed of immense sculptured letters which spell portions of the "Magnificat" and "Salve Regina." It is such a beautiful and unusual feature that one wonders it was not more often used. The letters have a flowing quality combined with considerable variation in shape which gives a pleasing note.

The tower is the culminating point in beauty as well as in height. It is generally compared to the papal crown with its triple tiers, but to eyes accustomed to the openwork spires of Spain it is especially reminiscent of that of Burgos. There is a similarity of shape and the same feeling of sky seen through interstices in the stone, though the actual motives are very different. In Caudebec the transition from the square of the foundation tower to the octagon of the next stage is achieved by means of a most unusual feature. Small, pierced arcs resembling tiny flying buttresses help both to support the height of the spire above and to make the change of shape less abrupt.

The interior seems small after the vastness of a cathedral, perhaps this very lack of size causes its intimate, sympathetic quality. The nave is simple, with round piers terminating in leafy capitals. In the spandrels small figures serve as brackets to support the engaged columns above. The delicate arches of the triforium are hurt by the balustrade which cuts into their height. The glass is fine, that of the south window especially so; this represents the Marriage of the Virgin, Joseph with his flowering wand and the unsuccessful suitor breaking his dead staff across his knee. A curious window depicts the Crossing of the Red Sea. The rushing waters which are engulfing the soldiers and horses of Pharaoh's army are of the most violent red color, a tone hardly convincing but one which casts a glorious glow on the gray stone.

The Lady Chapel is unusual, with two arches and a central column before it. The keystone of the elaborate vaulting is said to be the longest in the world. In the chapel is the tomb of the architect Le Tellier, willing apparently, like Gualdo of Troyes, to await the Day of Judgment beneath his handiwork.

One evening we walked along the river with the last sunset radiance staining the western sky and a moon riding high among clouds of silver brilliance. Perhaps it was on a night like this that William — not yet the Conqueror — came. He had fled from a plot against his life on the warning of a jester, a court fool, and he forded the Seine at Caudebec and eventually reached Arques. Since that time the town has had many royal visitors, some who besieged it and some who came on a mission of peace and recognition. St. Louis came to it in the thirteenth century and performed several notable miracles. In the fifteenth Charles VII made a spectacular entry into the city, where he was acclaimed with enthusiasm. Louis XI came to Caudebec and from it made a pilgrimage of penitence to a nearby shrine. He had need of forgiveness, this thin-lipped, cruel king whose narrow bigotry and fanatic faith had brought about such needless and terrible suffering. Louis XV brought Mme. de Pompadour here and they were received with every manifestation of loyal rejoicing, and Napoleon also paused here for a visit.

The kings and emperors of France are gone and Caudebec is a pleasant, bustling town where tourists and artists abound and where everyone is very busy about his own affairs. But every stone is storied, each street is a history, and the river is pure romance.

ROUEN

ROUEN is a city of churches and church bells. From every window a mounting spire can be seen, up every street one glimpses sculptured parts of ecclesiastical buildings, while the sound of ringing for the great services of life is heard at almost every hour of the day or night. We have usually stayed in the heart of the city, with the ceaseless sound of hurrying footsteps and voices pitched in every key in our ears. Early in the morning the cathedral bells chime gaily, tolling for the Mass with which the busy faithful or the most devout commence their day. These pass under our windows with the high sound of morning voices which seem to sleepy ears unusually clear and loud. In the evening the Angelus vies with the sharp, ceaseless ringing of the shrill bell of the cinema and the footsteps of the pious and of those in search of relaxation and amusement mingle in a steady stream towards the appointed goal of each and every one. One feels everywhere the dominating personal daily influence of this essentially churchly town.

We arrived in Rouen one afternoon too late for even a hasty view of the wonders of beauty we had come so far to see, before the inexorable demands of dinner claimed us, that most important and not to be evaded function of a French hotel. So it was evening, with a clear, white moon, when we walked down the narrow, busy thoroughfare under the Grosse Horloge which forms a bridge of time across the street, and came out upon the "place" before the Cathedral of Notre Dame. I shall never forget this my first sight of it in the moonlight. The curious stone of which it is built is rather soft and it has weathered into round, gentle contours washed chalky white on the upper surfaces by many rains and toned murky black in the sheltered spots by the settling soot and grime. In this silver light it was a startling study in black and white.

Our first visit to Rouen resulted in several drawings of this ever-tempting spot of architectural richness. The Tour de Beurre of the cathedral, which lifts its delicate head far above the workaday, noisy world, was a natural choice and the view which J. T. selected, looking up the narrow Rue d'Épicerie, showed this tower, the south transept and the much discussed iron spire above the crossing. The narrow street was hung with lengths of gaily colored cloth,

[48]

ROUEN

LACE IN STONE, ROUEN CATHEDRAL

Size of the original etching, 14¼ inches by 11½ inches

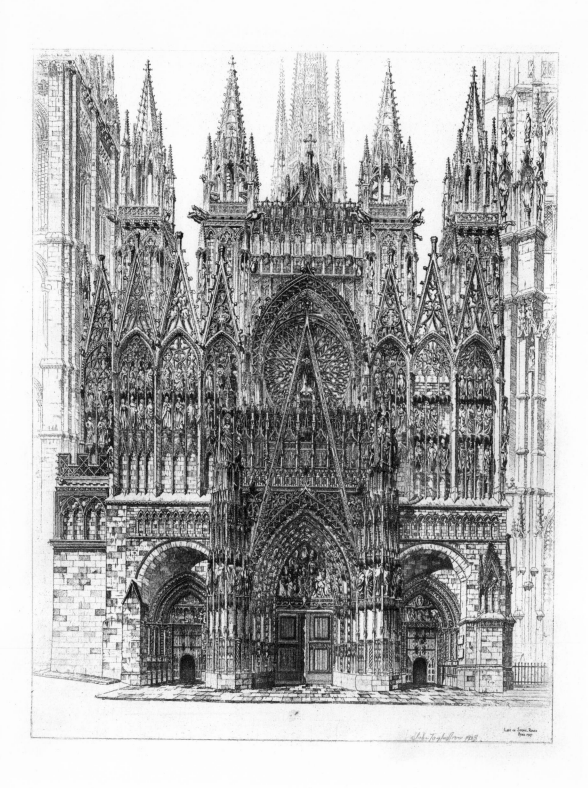

John Taylor Arms 1927   LACE IN STONE, ROUEN
                        APRIL 1927

for they sell material now instead of groceries in the little shops on either side. The arch of St. Romain not only made a frame with its pleasing curve but also afforded a much needed shelter at a season of sudden showers. Every year, from the platform above, a condemned criminal used to raise the reliquary of St. Romanus for the assembled multitude to see. The ceremony earned him his pardon and gave him back his life and liberty. The tower — marvel of sculptured masonry that it is — was built, stone by stone, detail by detail, from the money paid by the rich and self-indulgent for the privilege of eating butter in Lent. This is the origin of the name and it is curious to think of such a bit of spiritual exquisiteness existing because of frail mankind's unwillingness to forego that most transient of human enjoyments, the gratification of the sense of taste.

As the drawing grew and we studied the view before us, our feeling towards the iron spire underwent a considerable change. It might be much more pleasing; certainly it loses something by the nature of the material of which it is constructed, but it has a grandeur of height which gives it a distinct personal dignity. It dominates the city as well as the church by sheer strength and size and it is, after all, a perfectly logical expression in design and material of the commercial age to which it owes its being. I frankly prefer it to a slavish modern building which copies the Gothic forms and symbols of another generation but to whose creators the holiness and significance of them have long since lost all meaning.

From all over the city one sees this monumental flèche. In the old streets, where every house is mediaeval, where half-timber work and jutting gable become almost too commonplace for notice, it raises its turreted spire high into the sky. On street corners where the houses back up to each other at curious angles and ancient vines smother the roofs in tangled green, there too it dominates the scene with its message of modern times; and where the partially subterranean canals form the front yards of lines of homes, there also it makes itself felt with its black lines reflected in the half stagnant waters.

Of this cathedral of which so much has been written one hesitates to add one's personal word. It is a mixture of styles, as are so many; the façade is certainly too wide for true proportion and the towers are so dissimilar as to be almost jarring, but it is so marvellously beautiful in the workmanship and design of each portion that the sheer perfection of them unites all parts into a soul-satisfying whole. The Tour Romaine on the north is straight, severe and simple, with a paucity of detail in striking contrast to the elaborate fineness of its Gothic southern neighbor, in which delicate sculpture superimposed upon yet more delicate sculpture has resulted in a creation of spiritual refinement. The façade between these unlike towers is built about a central exquisite rose; there are twin turrets whose strength is masked by a spider web of Gothic tracery; a pediment in which not a square foot is left untouched by the sculptor's hand; and friezes of sainted figures full of life and movement whose canopies are chiseled with a delicacy that carries detail to an extreme. Here motives are carved upon other motives which are already so small in scale that one wonders there is thought, or need, or space for the yet more minute member. But somehow through it all there is a unity of plan, a rhythm of design which makes a whole, not alone harmonious, but sublime.

J. T. had an experience in connection with the cathedral which was unique to us as well as indicative of an unexpected art appreciation. For years he had wanted really to draw a church, not a spire here, an apse there or a distant bit seen over picturesque houses, but a whole façade, detail by detail. Of all the wealth of examples which France offered him he chose the most elaborate and the most highly ornamented, this one of Notre Dame. The matter was complicated moreover by the busy "place" over which this great monument holds sway and across which passes a great part of the traffic of this thriving, industrial city. There simply was no sequestered nook, no half sheltered corner into which he might withdraw himself in partial seclusion; only a small pavement too narrow to hold the jostling crowds who used it, parallel tracks on which the trams passed each other at frequent intervals, an "island of safety" perilously inadequate, and the open square into which came carriages and taxis, carts and great camions from four different directions. Beyond was the cathedral's façade — the perfect subject but a seemingly impossible one. The gendarme shrugged French shoulders and admitted that, if Monsieur chose to sit upon the little island, he would leave him in peace so long as he did not prove a dangerous impediment to traffic, but that he personally could guarantee no more. More seemed needed, so J. T. betook himself to see M. le Chef des Gardiens de la Paix de la Ville de Rouen. He found him as imposing as his title, a battle-scarred warrior with a gruff voice, whose only answer to each remark was a curt "Proceed." He finally gave verbal permission and four days of intensive work under the worst possible conditions succeeded. The passing traffic sent grit and choking dust on to the drawing and into eyes already half blinded by the glare, and heads cast black replicas of themselves which jerked confusingly across the white paper as their owners peered at it from different

[50]

ROUEN

"THE CROWN OF NORMANDY," ST. OUEN

Size of the original etching, $13\frac{1}{4}$ inches by $6\frac{3}{4}$ inches

John Taylor Arms - 1928 -

angles. People getting on and off the trams tripped over the knapsack and bumped against the stool in passing; poor things, they were in the right, not the artist, yet there was never an impatient word, only a gentle apology.

The drawing grew inch by inch, and day by day the store of amusing or pleasant incident increased. In France all natives feel that a stranger either speaks no French at all or so little that it hardly counts and all tourists are convinced that any artist willing to work in public must be some queer foreigner. In this way one collects some entertaining bits of opinion. Two girls stopped and one asked the other in high-pitched English tones, "I say, Ethel, do you think it's good?" Someone paused and a solitary head leaned over the paper. There was a moment's breathless silence, then an awe-struck voice whispered reverently, "My God!"

The daily tram commuters stopped morning and evening to congratulate Monsieur on the progress of his drawing and to cheer him on with words of encouragement as to the time still needed to complete it. A gentle lady hesitated and then asked if she might thank him for his interpretation of the cathedral, telling him rather breathlessly that she had been baptized, confirmed and married there and that she loved it more than any words could describe. The busy "buttons" from the hotel left his job three or four times a day and dashed to the square to check up on the progress made.

The fifth day had come with the end in sight, when a new gendarme, gold laced, important, conscious of his power, appeared and peremptorily ordered the artist from the scene as a menace to traffic safety. The latter pleaded permission. Where was it? Verbal? No good, get out! So J. T. went wearily once more in search of the Chief of Police. When he had told his tale the stolid warrior became galvanized into dangerous action. Telephone calls were sent and abrupt orders issued that Monsieur l'artiste Américain was under special protection and not to be molested by anyone! Joyfully J. T. started back, only to be stopped by the request that the drawing be shown to the Chief. The latter studied it carefully, said that he had been daily to the square to watch the work, then, looking up suddenly from under beetling brows, demanded "how he called himself." J. T. gave his surname, when to his intense surprise the other added the other two names, then smiled and with a courteous bow informed him that he owned two of his etchings. He had bought them out of his small salary because he liked them and because he cared for the city in his charge.

It is that love of the beauty in their own country, that understanding of another's appreciation and interpretation of it, that makes France the Mecca for all artists. In it they feel a sensitive response, not just to the concrete result of their efforts, but to the spirit which prompted their creation.

St. Maclou with its five portaled, projecting porch, almost unique in design, is a magnificent church and I found its adjacent cloisters quite as interesting. The galleries about this court have narrow bands of wooden sculptures, appropriately named the Dance of Death. This was once a cemetery and skulls and spades, bones and the grave digger's pickaxe, have been combined into a lovely, if grewsome, pattern.

One of the most beautiful and certainly one of the most satisfactory churches I know is that of St. Ouen. It is easy to forget the modern façade, whose deep gray stone suggests the cast iron facings of the nineteenth century hotels, in the perfection of the proportions of the building as a whole. About the roof runs a balustrade, within the safe confines of which one can walk around the church for a nearer study of the central tower and for a distant view over the city and to the circle of surrounding hills. They were doing some reconstruction when we were up there and we had an opportunity to look in at the great space between the roof and vaulting, to watch them fitting pieces of stone into the masonry and replacing sculptures by new copies. Seeing the quantity of modern figures which had been put in place gave us an idea of the extraordinary number of the original statues. The new ones seemed few indeed in comparison with the countless hundreds which had better withstood the ravages of time.

We looked down into the emptiness of the Hotel de Ville through the ancient beams blackened by a recent fire, down into the garden where Jeanne d'Arc was forced to abjure the miraculous quality of her vision, and over to the modern market where only a simple stone marks the place of her martyrdom. From here we could see the innumerable churches and belfries of the city, the Tour St. André, the churches of St. Vincent and St. Patrice, and in the distance St. Gervais, another claimant to the honor of being the oldest Christian building in France.

But the loveliest object in our range of vision was the lantern over the crossing, an extraordinary example of the most highly wrought, highly finished Gothic. In the square sides are windows of elaborate tracery; from the corners rise slender turrets, their outlines frosted with delicate sculptures; and the whole is surmounted by an octagonal motive finished in upright points. They call it the Crown of Normandy and with every reason. It suggests a master-

ROUEN
AN OLD CORNER, ROUEN
Size of the original etching, 6 inches by 4 inches

John Taylor Arms 1925

piece of the goldsmith's art which loyal workmen chiseled and engraved and set with precious jewels until it became a worthy symbol of their sovereign's rank and dignity. This is no king's crown, heavy with imperial power, but a queen's diadem, a tribute of the spontaneous love of her subjects.

Our way took us down from the roof and about the triforium where we could study the glass from near at hand and glory in its glowing colors. Then down again and out into the cool, pure nave. To me this interior suggests a pool of limpid water into which one may look deeply without encountering any impediment. The lofty columns carry out the idea, with a feeling of slender trees lining long banks, and the vaulting is of the smoky blue of an Indian Summer day. Into this church one could take a troubled heart or mind and be confident of a healing message, for the purity is not sterile coldness, nor the soaring height aloofness. It is the essence of spiritual development, the epitome of unclouded thought warmed by the sympathetic, mystic touch of love.

CHARTRES

IN eastern churches devout worshipers remove their shoes as a sign of respect, while in Christian churches men doff their hats and Roman Catholic women cross themselves reverently. In the heart of one to whom these forms are denied there is a longing for some expression of awe in the presence of Chartres Cathedral. It is so sublime in its architecture, so intellectual in its conception and, above all, so spiritual in its feeling that the need becomes acute to show by some concrete sign, or by some time-honored symbol, the realization that one is in the presence of greatness.

Master minds have interpreted its hidden meanings, great pens have written of its beauties and saintly souls have elucidated its religious position, but for each individual who comes humbly to the doors of this great cathedral there is a message waiting, new and vital because it is a personal message to each and every one.

The preponderant part of the world is rather mediocre, whether we think of architecture or of mankind. Most people have little faults or little virtues which are differently accented but which in the aggregate make of them average human beings, no better and no worse than the rest of humanity. Some are noticeably below this great strata and a few are outstandingly above it. In an individual of the latter type there is a ripened intellectual and spiritual fineness which makes friendship with him a harvest of enrichment. At first one may feel drawn to him by the force and beauty of his character, but only years can suffice to give a little insight into the true depths of his being. Each day, each hour of friendship deepens that knowledge and appreciation until one realizes that time cannot exhaust the endless possibilities of a beautiful human soul.

So it is with cathedrals. We like this one for one reason, that one for another, but in the very great examples there is a concentration of loveliness which raises them far above the average. Notre Dame at Chartres stands out preëminently; it is the flowering of the Gothic style, beyond the perfection of which man has never gone. One may fall under its spell at the first glance — most people do — but it needs years of study to appreciate a little the profundity of its meaning and the reason for its overwhelming beauty. Each day brings a revelation of unsuspected glories, each hour a better understanding of their place in the whole scheme. The greater one's equipment, the more this church has to give; the greater one's demands upon it, the more abundantly does it offer itself. It is an architectural miracle, a perennial spring of wonder.

The western façade is so imposing in mass that one forgets the detail, and so exquisite in detail that mass seems a secondary consideration. It combines such a hair-fine balance between the two, such a just proportion of strength and delicacy, that it forms the perfect whole. The complete blending in which no one side is given undue weight over another satisfies us more thoroughly than any other thing in nature or in art. We were created for poise and balance in our bodies, in our minds and in our souls. We have strayed far from that first ideal, but whenever we encounter it, under whatever form, it strikes a responsive note which vibrates to the very depths of our being.

People ask what is beauty and discuss the rules of its measurement. They quote other times and other places to prove that there is no standard for judging it. I believe that beauty lies in proportion, and that we appreciate this proportion in exact ratio to our own ability to keep a sense of balance. A race of ascetics could not have built Chartres, the blank, bare meeting houses of the Puritans prove that fact. It took a people in whom the normal, natural joys of life were strong and splendid, yet in proportion to their religious spirit and their self-sacrifice. Later, when the cult of beauty for itself alone went beyond the due balance of structural strength, architecture declined because the people had lost their subtle feeling for values.

So Chartres by its trueness is a great achievement and through the ages people have responded to it. We may not know why it fulfills our rarely satisfied need for supreme loveliness, but the proof is there in the generations who have acknowledged its perfection.

It is difficult, almost impossible, to be specific about this great cathedral within the narrow confines of a few words. The details, the history-soaked precincts, the priceless sculptures and radiant windows are books in themselves, the pages of which are open for our perusal and delight. It is the effect of the church as a whole which lingers, a stupendous manifestation of man's imagination. It is hard to realize that it was constructed stone by stone and mortared line by mortared line; it seems rather to have grown miraculously on its site. There are plenty of legends to support this feeling, in which the truth is as marvelous as the half truth.

The hill on which the cathedral is constructed contained a grotto for Druid worship in the days of long, long ago. Here they are said to have venerated "a virgin who should bear a child." Where did their belief end and the Christian version begin? Was it a premonition, or the echo of some ancient Jewish prophecy? There are tales of their coming in solemn procession with white bulls for the sacrifice, boys in spotless raiment, bards, priests and the Druids bearing bread, water and an ivory hand, symbol of justice.

On the site of that ancient, so-called pagan shrine the early Christians raised the first humble shelter for their new faith. And again they worshiped a Virgin and her Child. The chain has been unbroken through the ages and one feels in this cathedral of Notre Dame the endless sequence of thought and the gradual growth and development of man. It is against nature for things to change abruptly; the greatest upheaval needs time to be felt at any distance, and so it is with religion. However new and revolutionary a doctrine may be, yet it builds on the foundations of an earlier faith and becomes blended imperceptibly with certain of its attributes. The Madonna of Chartres stretches a friendly hand across the years to the Virgin of the Druids.

The building of the cathedral was attended by many miraculous events, while the actions of the human beings were as strange and as divinely inspired. When fire necessitated an almost complete reconstruction of their beloved church, the devoted people turned themselves into workmen of all classes. Those with training gave of it freely, while the unskilled harnessed themselves to carts and dragged stone from the distant quarries. As they worked they sang, or prayed, or confessed their sins. No one might work who did not bring a clear conscience to the task, and if one did by chance and was discovered, his burden was thrown aside and he was banished ignominiously. They camped by the carts when night overtook them and the Virgin appeared to them with words of encouragement and approval which stimulated them to further endeavor on the morrow.

The construction of this cathedral is the finest example of coöperation. With a single burning idea in mind, spurred on by a firm belief in the definite personal efficacy of their labors, the builders were united into an irresistible force. Paid workmen could not have accomplished the same result, it took the spontaneous offering of loving toil to achieve the miracle.

Who can describe the interior of this church? There is such a wealth of beauty that one is bewildered and overwhelmed by its force. The windows alone would fill a book, and still justice would not be done them. They date

John Taylor Arms 1928

largely from the thirteenth century and form one of the most complete and valuable series in existence. In them abound history and legend and conventional patterns, but greater even than these is their glorious coloring. Every tone and every half tone of the entire spectrum adds its iota to the designs of jeweled brilliance which lie like a prismatic tapestry on the gray stone pavement. The interior is vast and impressive, the sculpture is restrained and the great windows with their flaming, pulsating depths contribute the necessary warmth and color.

Deep in the earth is the famous crypt, the largest in France and the one most rich in ancient story. Here was the site of the primitive Druidic rites and later the Christian altar to "Notre Dame Sous-Terre," the oldest and most venerated of them all. And here, during the three days when fire was destroying the cathedral, some devoted priests guarded the most sacred relics and the reliquary containing the veil of Mary presented by Charles the Bald to the shrine which he considered the holiest of the many erected in her honor. This conflagration of 1194 was a great blow to the people who for generations had given of their best to their cathedral. They were about willing to renounce the project of rebuilding, feeling that an evil destiny hung over it. Their bishop endeavored to encourage them but in vain. When, after three days, the soot-blackened figures appeared through the smoke and ashes bearing their precious burden, then the people realized that a good, not a malign, fate was watching over them. They turned to the work with new courage and enthusiasm and in 1210 the cathedral was finished. At the service of dedication a shining light dimmed that of the candles and a great noise like that of thunder drowned the voices of the people at prayer. The awe-struck congregation felt that the Madonna had visited her loved shrine and had found it good.

This is a cathedral which should be seen often and under every condition of light; only so can one hope to gain a composite picture of its beauty. We have seen it under a hot July sun when every crocket, every detail was clear and defined against a hard blue sky. We have seen it during a thunderstorm when the lightning flashed greenly over sculptured surfaces and we feared a repetition of the destructive force which had already humbled this proud church. We have seen it in the rain, that fine rain of France which, like a silver veil, shrouded the building in soft luminosity, blurring the outlines with a delicate touch.

The Cathedral of Chartres has given us priceless memories of loveliness and it has more and yet more waiting for us to gather when we are next permitted a sight of its perfections. We do not, we cannot know it fully. Such slight knowledge as we have of it is based on three pilgrimages made in search of the message it might have for us. Our spirit was as reverent as that of the old-time pilgrims and we received the boon we had come to seek. Notre Dame granted us a vision as true as any of legend or miracle, a vision of sublime, transcendent beauty.

CHARTRES

A SAINT, CHARTRES

Size of the original etching, 5$\frac{3}{16}$ inches by 1 inch

A Saint

Chartres

John Taylor Arms 1919

MONT ST. MICHEL

TO write even intelligently of Mont St. Michel one must be either an architectural specialist or one who has given years to intensive study of the history and complicated construction of this extraordinary masterpiece. Everything has been said which can be said and there is no new note to strike, no further contribution to make. It remains, therefore, for us who have loved and lived with its sublime detachment, if only for a few days, to humbly record if we will our personal experiences or reactions, but not to attempt any real description of a monument well-nigh indescribable.

In my storehouse of remembered things three architectural silhouettes stand out preëminently — one is of the New York skyline, rising mountain-like with peaks and crags of gigantic buildings — one of San Gimignano, its rude, high towers dark against the blue — and one of Mont St. Michel.

This cone shaped rock springs boldly from a vast sea of sand which only the highest tides now cover. About its base the old fortified wall runs in an undulating, unbroken line. The houses of the tiny town cling so closely to the steep sides of the hill that they do not mar the outline of it, in fact they only serve to make the whole more solid, more compact. Crowning all is the church with its slender central spire. The great foundation of rock and town and abbey seems to surge to this culminating point. Needlelike, it cleaves the sky incisively, and all the great structure beneath it becomes merely a mounting base, a mass of upward-sweeping lines to support and hold this aspiring feature.

I realized the utter individuality of this silhouette when I first came to Mont St. Michel. The train followed the Normandy coast and I strained my eyes for a glimpse of the famous place. We came to a deeply indented bay and there it was across the wide expanse of water and sand. It might have been a model, it was so perfect in its smallness, but model or reality, no other combination of nature and man's handiwork resembles it even remotely. In fact it is so characteristic of itself that I, for one, felt a shock of surprise that anything could actually be so exactly as I had expected it to look.

But in every other way it far outstrips one's imagination. It is so beautiful, so complicated, so soaked in history that it is a bewildering thing. Even the first step inside the ancient wall is an experience. The entrance is through the old Burgher's Gate where, during the centuries of pilgrimages, those desiring admission must submit to an examination for weapons and dangerous implements. Persons of high degree were exempt until they reached the King's Gate, where everyone, regardless of rank or wealth, must give his reasons for coming and his intentions. For this was the wealthiest and the most influential of all mediaeval shrines. Wars were fought about it, and plots and campaigns and intrigues without number concerned themselves with schemes for its possession. At one time it was decided that the little river of Couësnon, which divides Normandy and Brittany at this point, should determine the ownership of this much disputed island, but that idea was abandoned as the low shore is so little above the level of the sea that the course of the river changes rapidly, and one year the Mont might find itself in one province and the next in another. It was finally conceded to Normandy, to which it still belongs.

The Abbey was founded in 708, following a vision in which St. Michael appeared to the bishop of Avranches and asked that an oratory should be built in his honor on the summit of this granite heap. The church grew, a Benedictine monastery was founded there and the fame of its miracle-working shrine increased and spread through the land. Famous visitors came from far and near, kings endowed it with gifts of money or precious relics, the monks waxed in power and influence and a little town grew up in the shadow of the abbatial walls. Fortifications were built and strengthened and increased until it became a stronghold without peer. What attacking troops could hope to cross the wide expanse where quicksands threatened to suck them to a slow and hideous death or the inrushing tides to engulf them in a quicker, more merciful drowning? And even if they braved these perils and reached the Mont, there were high walls and massive gates guarded by the belligerent townspeople, fighting for their very existence.

Through war and peace the pilgrims came. Nations might strive and plot or be at rest, but the physical and spiritual needs of the human unit went on, immensely important to each individual. The quantity of votive offerings increased steadily year by year and the wealth and strength of the order grew proportionately. Too much power is an evil thing for man or organization, and trouble and corruption crept close to the sanctuary. In the seventeenth century the Benedictines were replaced by a new brotherhood, but their prestige was gone and the buildings were later converted into a prison. Terrible tales are told of the iron cage, the lengthy incarcerations, the oubliettes and the prisoners who turned the great treadmill to provide power for the elevation

[60]

MONT ST. MICHEL
SUNRISE, MONT ST. MICHEL
Size of the original aquatint, 6⅜ inches by 7⅜ inches

SUNRISE, MONT ST. MICHEL
Size of the original aquatint, 6⅜ inches by 7⅜ inches

John Taylor Arms 1919

of food and water and supplies to this colony far above the sands. The treadmill is mute evidence of the reality of one of these stories, but many of the others have been proven false or exaggerated. This "Bastille of the Sea" was probably no better and no worse than the generality of prisons of that age.

The prisoners are gone and the pilgrims are tourists now, that ubiquitous and unpleasant class of people whose presence mars the greatest monuments. We all despise them as a whole, without a thought that — after all — we belong to them also! Here both the quantity and the type are appalling, and the little island is so small that they seem to rush in upon it as irresistibly and with as inundating an effect as the great tides which rise and surround it twice in every day.

We spent many nights there and found it the only way in which we could recapture a little of the lonely beauty and grandeur which are the rightful attributes of the place. All too soon the moving trains come rumbling across the causeway, the great busses unload their crowds of busy trippers, while the private cars are parked for yards and yards upon the sands. Then begins the sound of countless footsteps, the resounding tread of English feet planted solidly and firmly step by step, the click of fast moving American high heels, and the soft squeak of the rubber soles affected by the French for sight-seeing. The voices are as varied; deep tones, shrill tones, soft voices and loud, quick speech and slow speech, all combined into a ceaseless hum which makes this once quiet town a veritable beehive. The ramparts are lined with restaurants and cafés, and the waitresses, quick-witted from long experience, cry their wares to the passer-by according to his or her nationality. When a party of Americans appears on the horizon the call is, "Ice cream, Mister or Madam, or a little orangeade, very cold?" For the English, "Have your cup of tea here, don't go by us without taking your five o'clock." For the French, "A little apéritif before your dinner, here is the place for your liqueur."

J. T. had ample opportunity to hear this modern type of street call for he had picked a most peculiar place in which to work. Because of the unusually steep pitch of the jutting rock, it is difficult to draw the church as a whole unless one goes out on to the sands and takes in the entire town as well. He preferred a nearer and more detailed view, so he finally selected a spot on the ramparts from which he could see the church above him as well as the only group of mediaeval houses left standing by the destructive hand of modernism. If he had placed his stool on the walk, none too wide at best, he would have been stepped on, tripped over and sworn at by the swarms of sight-seers winding their way along the narrow chemin de ronde. Fortunately for him there was a deep embrasure in the wall, and into that he retired as a snail into its shell. The position had its disadvantages; it was so low that, after drawing one day from six in the morning until half-past three in the afternoon, he emerged from his niche with a stoop which threatened to become chronic. As he was facing due west and looking up besides, it was impossible to work between three or a little after and half-past five, when the sun became sufficiently hidden by the buildings to make drawing possible once more. Those hours we spent in the church trying to understand and absorb a little of the wonder of which there is such an overpowering amount that a lifetime could not suffice for its appreciation.

Because of the crowds and the vastness of the building and its various ramifications, it is necessary to see it under the supervision of a guide, herded along like a group of more or less docile sheep. J. T. had spent considerable time and trouble getting a permit in Paris to draw the "Monuments Historiques" and the moment seemed to have come to realize something on that effort. We were told by the head guide what to do, instructions which we dutifully obeyed. We joined a group waiting to go in, explained our intention to the cicerone in hushed whispers, then when we reached the terrace built out beyond the western front of the church we stayed behind, taking care that no one should see our lingering. So far so good. J. T., sketchbook in hand, began a drawing of the austere façade, gray, dark and patched so curiously with a bright brown lichen, while I sat and looked and dreamed or, turning my back on the man-made miracle of loveliness, walked to the wall around the terrace and looked down upon the sands far below me. A few hours before the sea had foamed about the foot of this rocky islet, then had retreated to such a distance that it now seemed merely a blue, shimmering line along the horizon. Finally, wishing to refresh my memory about some detail of the church interior, I strolled across the open space, opened one of the great doors and peeped in. What was my horror to find another party coming through, all gazing soulfully at the spot upon which the guide was discoursing. Hoping I had not been observed, as I was in no mood to explain my presence to anyone as officious and exasperating as most petty officials are, I gently closed the door and retraced my steps with the most innocent expression I could command adorning my countenance. But it was no use, the portal opened abruptly behind me and a small and irascible being demanded by whose permission and by what right I found myself there. I mentioned the magic permit, but his official dignity had been outraged and only the evidence of his own eyes could satisfy him. I waved to J. T., who held out the paper in one hand while he drew with the other, and then he had to believe us. He growled and grumbled, but a paper is a sacred thing to a Frenchman and we were left in peace.

Near us was the Saut Gautier, named for that poor prisoner called mad but perhaps most truly sane, who leaped to his death here, preferring that to further incarceration, while the very wall upon which we sat had a somewhat similar story. When the Revolution came the treasures of this monastery became the property of the state and of the people. Two men, one in charge of the proceedings and the other a jeweler from a nearby town, sat upon the terrace one day evaluating and listing the confiscated material. Much of it consisted of the Ex Voto offerings which were of all forms and sizes but among which the heart-shaped ones were the most popular. Some were gem-studded, some of gold or silver, many of copper, but each contained a little paper on which had been recorded the answered prayer which the offering commemorated. The jeweler noticed that his superior was trembling and, asked to get help, he departed, leaving the other alone with a little metal heart in his hand. The initials on it were his own, the parchment it enclosed bore the names of his parents and their expression of thanks for the life of their only son. He suddenly remembered an accident of childhood, the agonized suffering, the doctor's despair, then the pilgrimage made by his mother and father on bare feet to Mont St. Michel, many hours walk away. He remembered his cure and their rejoicing, and, trembling and sobbing, he walked to the wall of the terrace. A moment later his inanimate body lay at the foot of the cliff, his hand still holding close the little heart.

As the shadows lengthened we joined still another group and made our way out with them, seeing once more the various rooms, the structure upon top of structure that make this building one of the great monuments, not only of France, but of the world. From its founding until it was abandoned as a prison in 1863 there have been new constructions and changes without number. One building replaced another or new units were added to those already there until the whole summit of the Mont was covered by this complicated mass, a perfect honeycomb of superimposed masonry. Each portion is a stone book of architecture or history for one with eyes to read and understand. Each room is a story for one with ears to hear.

It would take a volume even to touch the surface things in this extraordinary building. Prominent in my memory are certain features which come back to me as clear images of beauty with the mention of Mont St. Michel. One is of the Crypt des Gros Piliers, with its enormous columns from which rises the simple, massive vaulting unbroken by capital or sculptured motive. One is of the Salle des Chevaliers, a mighty hall of graceful arches. Here Louis XI instituted the coveted Order of St. Michel in the fifteenth century and here the monks worked at the exquisite illuminated manuscripts and missals for which they were so famous. The hall is cool in summer and must have been tomblike in the bleak and bitter winter months. How could their blue and swollen hands hold brush or pen with sufficient steadiness to execute these marvels of delicacy? Perhaps their religious exaltation kept them warm. One is of the Cloisters, that one-time garden to which all the water had to be carried, for the island is arid as the sands about it. A double row of delicate pillars is a frame of frail loveliness about the now empty court. And one is of the aerial steps up to the exterior of the apse where, from an intricate web of flying buttresses, I could see for miles across the bay to the distant land, while above me towered the often lightning-struck, often replaced statue of the guardian angel of Mont St. Michel.

The days were times of work and noise and hurry, during which we tried to think consecutively and learn some of the fundamentals, some of the history and religion from which this glorious structure had sprung. But when evening came, and the last train and the last tourist-laden car had gone, then we renounced all conscious thought and let the beauty and the spirit of the place flow into us. We walked about the walls as the sun set in crimson splendor, then sat and watched the dying light across the sands. The salt marshes in the distance became a fringe of verdure towards which the pollard willows bent with curious convolutions, the sands turned pink, then lavender, then a bluish gray. Finally the moon came out, flooding the landscape with a cool radiance and touching the ancient buildings of the Mont with a silver light.

MONT ST. MICHEL

THE ABBEY CHURCH OF ST. MICHEL

Size of the original etching, 15¼ *inches by* 11⅞ *inches*

John Taylor Arms -1926-

LE MANS

LE MANS has always seemed to me an interesting example of the magnificent results obtained by the right use and elaboration of the means necessitated by certain physical defects. From time immemorial man has built his place of worship on the highest bit of land at his command, primarily that it might be just so much nearer to the heaven which had to him a definite as well as a spiritual location, and also that it might be more inaccessible to marauding foes. So when the great wave of ecclesiastical building swept France in the Middle Ages and the designers of Le Mans began the glorious cathedral which is one of the art treasures of the world, it was natural that they should erect it on the site of an older church in the center of the town which clung then, as now, to the steep sides of a hill rising from the river Sarthe. The design was a large one, for theirs was to be the great cathedral of the world, an ambition shared by all the other visionary builders of that time. The faith and dreams of many of them came true, partly because of their religious fervor and belief in their conceptions, but largely also due to the technical knowledge they possessed and their willingness to count time as nothing while they worked out on paper and in stone engineering problems which would often baffle modern science, and the artistic development of which they carried to a superlative degree.

Perhaps the architects of that long ago day regretted the dimensions of this hill on which they were to erect and later enlarge their ecclesiastical monument. Tradition having established the facing of a church, they found themselves with a ridge too narrow for the desired length of nave and choir. Undaunted, they constructed a terrace and built upon it an apse of surpassing beauty which rises in triple tiers, pierced by delicate, high, sharp-pointed windows and flanked by flying buttresses of surprising lightness. It seems a magnificent ship sailing into the east, buoyant and alive. Only Notre Dame and St. Étienne of Bourges are at all comparable to it, and I do not like to compare. Each is so perfect in itself and in its setting that I, for one, cannot analyze them coldly, but prefer to enjoy them to the fullest extent, one at a time.

The usual first vision of Le Mans is the one from the river-front where the close-built town rises sharply, mirrored in the quiet water, while above, the cathedral raises high shoulders and one massive southern tower over the surrounding roofs. Yet afterwards, when one has threaded the narrow streets and come upon the magnificent apse, sweeping with ascending lines up from its high terrace, this is the view which lingers in one's memory, and one feels that this, rather than the other, is the main façade of the cathedral. The west front is very different in character. It is hard to find and is reached by a mere blind alley which opens out into a small "place" before it. It is Romanesque and crumbling and the interesting geometric frieze above the main portal is weather-worn into blurred outlines. It seems far away from the busy town and the life of the present; ancient, remote, simple, very retiring, in striking contrast to the great size and bold free lines of the apse with its vitally dominating personality.

The interior shows almost as marked a transition in type of architecture and in age. The nave is not high, the aisles with blind Romanesque arcades are even lower. The arches of the vaulting were originally the round ones of the earlier period, though when the church was rebuilt in the Gothic style they were broken in each center and made slightly pointed. The effect is unfortunate, as the change was not radical enough; the low curve of the first Romanesque arch shows clearly at each side while the middle portion rises more sharply. The result is an outline in which both characteristics are seen, and in which each loses something of beauty and purity. Some of the windows of the nave have stained glass said to be the oldest in France, and the richness and harmony of the colors ably serve to substantiate the assertion. The western one is of particular beauty and interest, with its nineteen panels depicting the life of St. Julien, patron saint of the cathedral. There are various legends and suppositions about him. He was certainly the first archbishop of Le Mans, coming to Gaul from Rome as a missionary of great piety and fervor. Some say that before his conversion he was Simon the Leper whom Christ healed and later honored by taking a meal in his house, though between those first years of the Christian era and the third century, when, as Julien, priest and bishop, he is historically recorded in France, there seems to be an undue lapse of time indicating inaccuracy or a span of life unknown today. Whatever the truth, he lives on in the memorial window and in the church, the first seeds of which were planted by his burning faith.

The capitals still retain traces of color, and are mostly carved in a massive, vertical leaf design. I noticed an unusual motive in the north transept: below the windows, the stone tracery is formed by the use of the French fleur-de-lis

THE CATHEDRAL OF ST. JULIEN, AND THE OLD TOWN
Size of the original etching, 9¼ inches by 9¾ inches

John Taylor Arms 1927

instead of the usual Gothic trefoil, which lends a charming note of variety. The apse, here as on the exterior, is the focal point and beauty spot of the building. It is a choir of luminous, glowing glass, held lightly in place by slender shafts of moulded stone. It is delicate yet strong, colorful and dignified. There is a double ambulatory, the outer one with its fine windows forming one of the triple tiers, the next one, much higher, forming the second, and the third made by the central choir itself. Each one is pierced to the limit of structural strength by glorious windows. The lunettes above the triforium of the ambulatory are most unusual and especially beautiful, and in them, as well as in the other glazing, red predominates, casting a mystic purple hue upon the gray stone.

The different entrances to the cathedral interested me by their varying character. In addition to the west one, so venerable and worn, there was a little door leading from the north side of the choir. It appeared to be open, so I tried it and stepped out into a small green garden, empty so far as I could see, and so steep that I marveled at the tenacity of soil and roots which could cling at such an angle. I never learned what it was, or where it went. It seemed too peaceful and too private for exploring feet, so I withdrew and went to find what of interest and contrast the southern portal had for me. On my way a chapel in the apse arrested my attention. This was in honor of Jeanne d'Arc, and on each of its side walls was a marble tablet. One, dated September sixth, 1914, commemorated the vow made by the Archbishop of Le Mans to dedicate a chapel to the Warrior Maid if she would protect the cathedral and city under his care from the invading army. The other tablet, inscribed April seventeenth, 1921, showed the fulfilment of the vow. It was a little thing, yet it made the Church seem so alive, so much an integral part of daily modern life, not just the historic monument of a burned-out fervor as we so often consider it. This latter date was the third anniversary of the canonization of the much loved saint, and surprised me anew as I realized how very recently she had been so acclaimed officially. Only a few short years after her martyrdom she had become a venerated legend in the hearts of her fellow-countrymen, then a holy person whose humble origin and great courage made her seem nearer and more sympathetic to them than some of the older saints, whose experiences were those of a different age and whose virtues they could not hope to emulate. Many efforts were made to have her name inscribed on the calendar but the Church was loath to acknowledge her sanctity in view of the fact that it, as a body, had cast her off and countenanced her death. It is curiously hard for an individual to admit himself in the wrong, and it seems well-nigh impossible for an organization to do so. Although the mistake had been made centuries before, still the Church could not bring itself to acknowledge its culpability, and Jeanne d'Arc lived in the hearts of her people an unhaloed saint. The war came, bringing over four years of a never before dreamed-of intensity of mental and physical suffering. The world was a place of noise, mud, pain and horror. There came tales then of a shining armored figure which led the army of France, now as before, across the tortured soil to victory; stories of a light seen, and a comforting voice heard, by soldiers on the eve of a charge which brought them death, and awed whispers of bright visions in which the radiant Maid pointed the way to freedom from tyranny. No one will ever know how much these experiences, real or fancied, helped to buoy up spirits sorely tried by years of warfare, yet it is significant and just that five months after the signing of the Armistice, Jeanne d'Arc was canonized at Rome in a ceremony of such magnificence that it seemed an effort at compensation for its lateness. Now every church has a statue at least, many have a chapel in her honor, and she has finally come into her rightful place, a position long since accorded her by the affection of the people of France.

Our last egress was through the southern transeptal door. This is the most used of all, for a long line of stone steps ending in a double curved staircase descends from it to the busy street at the base of the apse. The sculpture on this portal is very fine and very old, with long lines of Byzantine drapery. The mutilation it suffered was never restored and the edges are crumbled and worn to a mellow softness. From here we had an inspiring view up the rugged, soaring side of the tower, at the base of which a delicate loggia adds a contrasting note of grace and lightness. And looking to the west we saw, on the Renaissance façade of the adjoining chateau, an interesting pattern of shadow cast by the little Gothic turrets of the cathedral.

GISORS

GISORS ranks as one of our mistakes, in spite of the fact that it is a quaint town containing the interesting church of St. Gervais and is beautifully situated in the great wheat and rye fields of fertile Normandy at a spot where three little streams join forces to become the larger river Epte. On a previous motor trip, somewhere between Coutances and Paris we had passed through a hilly town of narrow streets where a hasty upward glance, snatched between traffic needs, had revealed a church perched high above massed and mounting roofs. We had paused upon a perilous incline, had looked back at it and had registered it as one of those places to which we would come back "some day" when an inexorable steamer sailing date was less imminent. When planning our next church pilgrimage we pored over maps and books and happened upon Gisors, which sounded so familiar that we both came to the conclusion it was the "lost city" of which we could find no record in any of our note books. All the information seemed to point to a confirmation of our theory, so we blithely included its name in our tentative itinerary which rarely, if ever, remains in anything like the form in which it first appears. On a day of threatening clouds we roamed that general section, looking at several church towers which sorely tempted J. T.'s pencil, but always with the memory of Gisors, that charming hill town, to lure us farther on. When we arrived, there was no hill except the one on the outskirts crowned by Richard Cœur de Lion's castle and the church was far, far different from the one whose mental image we had treasured for so long. It was too late to go back over our route and a certain stiff-necked quality inherited from Puritan ancestry prevented us from giving in, and perseverance — or stubbornness — was ultimately rewarded by a really charming view of a very dull subject.

The most attractive thing about the town is the way the little streams — here trained into docile stone-walled canals — wind their way through the streets and below the crowding houses. To reach his front door or garden many a Gisors householder must cross a narrow iron bridge over fast-running water in which the long green river grasses trail far down stream in the swift current. Here the hides are washed and left to soak — a part of the process of tanning, which is the great industry of the town — and here the women come

[69]

with their bundles or baskets of clothes to kneel in the washing sheds, built at intervals along the banks, where they pound and rinse their linen clean in that most laborious and back-breaking way. Here too they dip up pails of dubious water with which we fear they cook, but hope they use for cleaning house, and into the same stream the busy housewife throws the contents of her various pots and pans. A mixed water surely, saved only by its speed from being a public menace.

Along one of these picturesque canals, almost directly in front of the most lovely of all carved mediaeval houses, J. T. took up his position with a pleasant line of jumbled roofs before him and the east end of the church with its curious belfry rising over them. But that and the north portal proved to be the only really good features. The west façade is of a peculiarly hideous epoch of the Renaissance and has not even beauty of setting, sunk as it is far below street level with only a small, barren, open space before it. Its severe rectangularity rises grudgingly into a northern tower of heavy motives. The south portal is very plain and opens upon a bare and ugly street, while the northern one is so hemmed in that one can only see its beauty framed between the overhanging houses of an alley so narrow that one has the impression of looking out through an archer's slit in a fortified wall. The detail of this door is remarkably delicate; I have never seen such minutiae of carving except in the cathedral of Rouen. The Gothic canopies under which stood statuettes, before the artistic cataclysm of the Revolution, are a marvel of stone cutting. The motives of an entire building are here reduced into a space only a foot or two high, making each cusp, each crocket, each openwork tracery appear like a miniature model for a Gothic builder. I personally feel that the scale has been so cut down that there is a distinct lack of harmony between the door and its massive and severe background, but other opinions disagree and consider it so jewel-like in its exquisiteness that it can well dispense with an elaborate setting. The massive carved wooden doors are fine.

The interior of this remarkable edifice is very curious. A trusty guide book, which we consult largely for maps, cautiously classes it as a building in which "one may study the various phases of architecture with interest and profit." This may be so, but somehow I prefer to form my opinions of these different types by the best examples of each which can be found, rather than by one building in which the three principal styles are represented — as well as their transitional periods — in such confusion that each of them detracts seriously from the other two. The plan is neither cruciform nor quite otherwise.

GISORS

CHURCH OF ST. GERVAIS

Size of the original pencil drawing, 10 inches by 8⅝ inches

CHURCH OF ST. GERVAIS
Size of the original pencil drawing, 10 inches by 8$\frac{5}{16}$ inches

John Taylor Arms 1928

In reality it is a long rectangle with a very slightly rounded chapel for the apse, while lateral chapels, built the length of the nave, narrow the effect of the interior and leave the exterior unchanged. In the last bay before the choir these chapels have been eliminated and the effect makes a sort of false transept. The western end is Renaissance, heavy and square in feeling; the nave is mostly Gothic, with two twisted columns in the south aisle which are purely Byzantine. A gallery about the transepts has a simple, strong balustrade resting upon a triple moulding equally wide and so deeply and elaborately carved as to make a most disturbing line. The glass is very fine and the painted panels about the altars in the east end are extremely interesting. They date from 1603 and depict the lives and miracles of St. Gervais and St. Portais (to the former of whom the church is dedicated) as well as scenes from the life of Christ. The colors have remained surprisingly true and luminous and the drawing is good and full of movement and life. In the two adjoining panels where the twin saints are brought — their hands bound behind them — before Count Astase, who sits enthroned with his advisors and courtiers about him, there is considerable drama and a definite effort at the portrayal of characters and faces rather than the simperingly sweet types which that age and generation usually depicted as the only expression of holiness. There is a naïve quality in the architecture represented; for instance in the Nativity scene St. Joseph is shown leaning against a Corinthian pillar and the manger from which an undersized cow and donkey placidly feed is built out from the massive wall of a towered castle.

About the town of Gisors history throws a magic spell of association with Richard Cœur de Lion, who was finally forced to surrender his castle on the hill to Philip Augustus in 1196 and who then sorrowfully built his new Château Gaillard at Les Andelys as a pitiful sop to his injured vanity. Walter Scott must have gotten much of his data here, and woven some of his most poignant tales of ancient chivalry about these ruins. We drove one day to Beauvais for a refreshing and satisfying hour or two in that well-nigh unbelievable building, and came home through the late afternoon towards the setting sun whose rays shone in long horizontal lines between heavy clouds. In the fields the August harvest had been stacked in golden cones, starring the meadows, or, with the grain safe stored against the winter, the straw was being built into huge round piles, high as houses. The method of ploughing, planting and harvesting, even the shape of the stacks, is the same as it was when Richard lived here and went hunting in the surrounding forests, still famous for their game. The towns are a little bigger and the roads are very much better but the country and the people are little changed. As we drove along, our eyes filled with beauty and our minds with history and legend, a very extraordinary light effect took place, unlike anything I have ever seen. The meadows on our left were green with lines of trees in full summer foliage but the clouds so changed the light that everything was turned a hard, leaden green of foreboding hue. On the right, the fields were those from which the wheat had so recently been cut and the stubble was golden in the late light as far as eye could see and even the cattle that grazed upon the scanty growth remaining were of a pale brown variety which toned in perfectly. It made me think of those queer things found on the heights of hills or buildings where a blue glass shows the scene as it might be in winter, a yellow one as it might be in summer and I forget what else; only in this case we had a scene of warm sunlight on our right and one of threatening storm upon our left, divided exactly by the bare white road of our passing.

QUIMPER

ON a sunny Sunday in July we started to cross Brittany from the north-eastern corner to that of the southwest. As this great province is especially noted for its picturesqueness, its natural beauties and curiosities and its historical interest, rather than for its architectural monuments, we were making it only a brief and hurried visit. We felt the Celtic quality as soon as we reached Basse Bretagne, which begins at St. Brieux: the names, the customs and the types were so characteristic of the inhabitants of Wales and many sections of Ireland that it was not at all surprising to find the great southwestern district called Cornouaille. It resembles its sister Cornwall in many ways, and they say that a Welshman can understand a Breton better than a Frenchman can.

The countryside in the inland section was primitive, bare and rude. There were great rolling uplands with black jagged outcrops of rock and poor fields of sparse, coarse grass walled by banks of stones and earth in which the gorse grew, putting forth prickly arms at wide and defensive angles. Here and there we came upon a little village of stone houses clustered about a single church. Everywhere there were roadside shrines and Calvaries, for the Bretons are the most devout of all French people. It was impressive to come upon a simple granite cross, as straightforward, sincere and strong as the men who constructed it, in an expanse of barren country with not a house in sight and hardly another sign of human nearness. Their religion and their personal expression of it is the dominant factor in the lives of this self-contained, superstitious, kindly race and it has marked their characters, their architecture and their habits with its individual stamp.

These Calvaries are a good example of this, and one finds them everywhere. Built of the deep gray stone of the region and sculptured with the naïve simplicity of a primitive people, they demonstrate a religious fervor which is their strongest racial characteristic. At Glomel we had our first view of a quite elaborate example. The church before which it stood was forceful, strong, uncompromising, weathered by time and the elements, but unchanged and unshaken. It resembled many other rural churches as we grew to know them but we remember it always as a particularly lovely one. It was ample

[73]

and sturdy, with the low roof line and broad western end making a wide-angle gable and a generous façade. The detail about the penetrations was delicate, in striking contrast to the other surfaces which were plain and unrelieved and broken only by small, infrequent windows. The crockets were strong and heavy, tufted by shaggy mosses into soft shapes. Before this dignified church and among ancient gravestones, stood the Calvary.

The landscape here was bleak and stern and full of contrasts. The great plains were sparsely settled by tiny, huddled hamlets. Often one entire town seemed made up of only one house, for each generation and its ramifications had built their new homes so closely to the ancestral one that, with the necessary barns and sheds and other farm buildings, they formed a single unit of considerable size and importance. In certain sections the country was almost bare of vegetation. Great black boulders broke the poor soil at frequent intervals and the meagre grass offered scanty sustenance to occasional herds of sheep. From this high plateau the views on either side were extended and magnificent.

Presently we found ourselves in a different land, with orchards and fertile fields and towns gay with the peasant population, who still cling to their garb of olden days. Every woman in Brittany wears the cap of her town and the men's hats are as varied and almost as universally worn, but the complete costumes have disappeared from the cities except for days of festival. Most of the dresses were black, though some were embroidered and some had bands of color about neck or skirt. The concentration of detail and of color was found in the aprons.

We wound our way down towards Quimper through an ever increasing crowd of brightly dressed people, until we reached the city and found ourselves by sheer good fortune in the midst of the famous Fête de Cornouaille. We watched the cortège from a balcony and thought it a little formal, a little arranged for the occasion, but the costumes were beautiful; each one was the most elaborate or the most picturesque of the town or county which its wearer represented.

In the evening there was folk-dancing to the droning sound of some pipes, the art of playing which is fast dying out. This was completely spontaneous, and young and old joined in with zest and enthusiasm. At first the music seemed to have no rhythm and the steps no particular sequence, then, as eyes and ears grew more accustomed, tune and time and dance emerged into a fascinating unity. As a whole, the men danced better than the women. The

QUIMPER

NORTH TOWER OF ST. CORENTIN

Size of the original pencil drawing, 13¼ inches by 5¼ inches

John Taylor Heins 1826

young girls were a little conscious of their conspicuous loveliness, of their snowy caps whose bows or streamers blew and fluttered about their heads, and of the frank admiration of the spectators. The young men danced with unconscious grace and abandon, some in the sailor suits of Concarneau, made from the same material as their red-dyed sails and with spreading berets on their heads; some in black with elaborate vests, orange embroidered or of somber velvet with long rows of antique silver buttons; while some in so-called "modern" garb wore lavender gray or pale blue, tight-fitting trousers, short dark coats and wide black hats with a large silver buckle at the crown.

The older people fascinated us even more. Both men and women danced with their hearts in it. One old lady especially appealed to us. Her dress was black, with a spotless collar stiff-starched and so finely pleated as to form a veritable ruche, and she wore a white cap with loops on either side. The face was tanned and wrinkled by exposure until it resembled a withered apple, with still a hint of healthy color in the cheeks. Her teeth were mostly conspicuous by their absence and she was bent and shrunken. She stepped out bravely in her worn button shoes, taking the shuffling step (which seems to be the fundamental one of all country dances) at the correct moment, turning and twisting with a certain gay dignity very lovely to watch. We felt that she had danced all her life because she loved it, that no matter how footsore and weary she might be after a hard day in the fields, the music of the pipes would always entice her into the midst of other tapping feet.

When a sober work-a-day world dawned the next day and confetti was swept up, booths packed and all the festive preparations put away for another year, we were surprised and pleased to find that the costumes persisted, even though in a modified form. On entering the Cathedral we found Mass just finishing. The nave was filled with kneeling figures, their white caps, like gigantic flowers, forming an almost unbroken mass and — to complete the illusion — these moved and bent as the service proceeded as if a wind passed over them.

St. Corentin began the building of the cathedral and it is dedicated in his honor as its first bishop. He seems to be a very local saint, as indeed many of the Breton ones are, honored and revered in certain towns or sections but not recognized officially by the Roman Catholic Church. The most conspicuous feature of his life was his miraculous fish, which reappeared each morning in the little pool of water beside his cell and which he caught and ate with equal regularity each evening. One finds the fish represented all over the church, in the carvings of the pulpit and in the stained glass, some of which dates from the sixteenth century and is very good. We were also amused to realize that this miracle was the reason for the mark of the fish found on the bottom of much of the Quimper pottery.

The color of the church interior is very lovely, a rich brownish gray with a hint of luminous rose in it, but the most conspicuous feature of all is unfortunate. The apses of most churches in France (and perhaps elsewhere) are apt to incline slightly to the north, due, some say, to the tradition that the head of the dying Christ fell towards His right side. Other authorities maintain that the lack of perfect alignment between choir and nave is due, partly to imperfect surveying instruments, partly to the fact that one portion was built at one time and the other later. Either a new nave was added to the old apse or a new choir was built to replace an earlier one. During the construction a temporary wall was raised between the two and a slight or even considerable variation in line might be a quite natural result. Those in favor of the first theory cite the fact that in only one or two instances does the variation occur towards the south.

At any rate, the choir of St. Corentin not only inclines but curves so decidely northward that the effect of perspective is appreciably marred. The central apsidal chapel, which is normally directly behind the high altar when seen from the middle door, is here so far to one side as to be cut by the pier of the first arch. It is a pity, for the nave is very fine, narrow and high and with a graceful triforium.

The exterior is completely satisfying and very characteristic of the sturdy, simple folk who built it. The twin towers rise with identical detail of vertical lines, up and up until one feels that the topmost point must surely pierce the blue and reach that heaven which is the daily thought and prayer of every Breton. Begun two centuries earlier, the towers were never completed until a few years ago, when the present very lovely spires were added. If the modern architects responsible for them had the original plans, then they were most conscientious in carrying them out, but if they lacked those plans and conceived and executed the spires from a loving study of the original building, then all honor is due them. The result of their thought and labor is so in keeping, so perfectly in harmony with the rest of the church that one feels no transition, merely a logical continuation. The long, pure lines carry through unbroken, the detail is severe, almost Norman as in Coutances, and from the sculptured portal to the slender tops of the spires is one glorious, upward-sweeping surge.

[76]

The views of the Cathedral were so interesting and varied from all over the town that it was hard to settle on only one. It was charming half glimpsed up one of the narrow streets of overhanging houses or with its towers seen above the close clustering roofs, or again at twilight, from the port, with masts in serried ranks as a foreground. J. T. finally decided on the view which showed the whole long slender length of one tower and a famous mediaeval house upon a foreground corner, with stories corbeled out to a perilous distance. Here he sat with his back to a ladder upon which another artist stood and painted a sign above him, dropping an occasional bit of paint upon the head beneath as he leaned over to look at the drawing. Like all the other Bretons we have met, the passers-by were so gentle, so kindly and always so perfectly dignified. They murmured low-voiced apologies as they squeezed by, they asked gently if they might look and voiced their comments in a few words of restrained admiration. They accepted this strange artist as an honored guest of the city and yet they must be bored by the sight of a paint box or sketch block. One incident happened, indicative of their feeling for coöperation. About the second day a woman living in a nearby house appeared with her very small boy and asked J. T., quite casually, if he would mind the child while she did an errand or two! Before he could collect his senses she was gone, leaving him in charge of a small morsel of humanity who might speak French but then again might speak nothing but Gaelic. However, having been told in a parting admonishment to stand still, he obeyed so implicitly that J. T. feared complete paralysis for him. He offered him a bit of eraser in lieu of a better toy, which so enchanted his charge that no further amusement was necessary.

I was interested to run across the story of Tristan and Isolde here, for Penmarch, a few kilometers away, is the traditional site of his castle. There he lay mortally wounded by poisoned arrows, waiting for his beloved to come over from Cornwall and cure him. Her coming was to be announced by the color of the sail upon her boat, an appropriate signal when one thinks of the sails along the coast. The fishing boats show blue, green, orange, red and all their tones and half tones, varied also by patches of brilliant and unfaded stuff. We did not see one of black, the color which Tristan dreaded and which the other Isolde, she of the White Hands, reported falsely as the one upon the boat instead of the white sail which streamed in the breeze, bearing Isolde of the Golden Hair to her lover.

Brittany also naïvely claims King Arthur and his Round Table as its own, though with what reason I could not discover. There are various local versions of their adventures and the legend of the Holy Grail is one often encountered.

Our only other pause in Brittany was at Vannes, a fascinating town in every way except for the cathedral. That was a great disappointment. Badly placed, crowded and built into narrow streets, its fine high roof is spoiled by the lack of a tower and its exterior is crumbling and mutilated. The apse piles up well but lacks a focal point or foreground, so J. T. regretfully abandoned it and turned his eyes and his pencil towards a strictly secular subject. There was enough of interest in and about the town to keep one busy for weeks. The great Pardon at Ste. Anne d'Auray took place at this time, so that some of us were able to see that most sincere and unaffected religious festival. There is an ancient saying: "Mort ou vivant, dit-on, à Sainte Anne une fois doit aller tout Breton."

Ste. Anne, Mother of the Virgin, is the patroness of all those who follow the sea and her shrine is an especially sacred one to the seafaring folk of this long, dangerous coastline. Here they come, all who can, year after year to pray for the safety of those they love who spend such a great part of their lives on the water, and also to pray for the souls of those whom the sea has taken. The Bretons are an especially devout race and the cult of the dead is one particularly dear to them. This is noticeable everywhere, in their folklore, in their churches, in their Calvaries.

On the way to Josselin, with its château constructed on the living rock, its Renaissance towers cleverly conforming to the natural contours and seeming to rise from a surf-washed shore, with its church built to house the miracle-working statue of Notre Dame du Roncier and with interesting wooden vaulting, we stopped at Gehenno to see the Calvary there, one of the most interesting in Brittany. It stands in the cemetery to the south of the church, with a low ossuary behind it consisting of two half subterranean moss-covered rooms containing many bones and one or two statues. The Calvary is very high, fully twenty feet. There is a double cruciform base of dark gray stone, on the face of which is a low bas-relief of the Entombment and about which are grouped several figures. On the front part of the base is a knight on horseback, his sword in his hand, facing the figure of the Christ carrying His cross. Farther back is another group consisting of the Virgin with the dead body of her Son in her arms and saints and apostles on either side. Three crosses rise behind this, those of the robbers lower and to the right and left, that of Christ in the center with a statue of Mary and one of St. John on a small base partway up the shaft

CHAPEL OF ST. AVÉ

Size of the original pencil drawing, 6⅞ inches by 7½ inches

of the cross. A pair of figures hard to define are twined around the base and seem to be part of the Descent from the Cross. The conception is very naïve, with so many different events shown simultaneously and with no obvious demarcation, but it is remarkably beautiful in composition and full of a sincere and devout fervor.

J. T. was anxious to add to his collection a drawing of one of the very characteristic small churches of Brittany. St. Avé had been described as an "église absolument délicieuse," so we started in search of it one evening of threatening storm clouds. Our directions had been vague and when we paused to ask questions local pride directed us up a hill to a crowning church which nearer inspection revealed as new and uninteresting. It was growing very dark as we retraced our steps and when we finally discovered our objective, night had fallen and there was a hint of distant thunder.

The little building was well worth the effort of reaching it. It is a small church, compact and solid. It nestles comfortably behind high walls which guard its surrounding graveyard, in the midst of which is a Calvary of unusual form. The one deep door is simple and strong, with a plain round window above it. The only note of lighter ornament is found in the crockets which outline the gable; these turn up with an engaging quirk which makes of them a thoroughly charming feature. It is a country church built for and by a people who needed its help and who love its simple beauty.

We had turned the lights of the car on the church to help us see it and so a sudden drop of rain was our first warning that the storm was upon us. We left St. Avé hastily, and as we hurried back through fitful flashes of lightning and heavy rain, and with the thunder rolling about us, we felt in the very center of one of the oldest and most fascinating of Breton legends. It had just been told us and the memory of it was vivid. This tale is not only characteristic of the occult Breton mind but it also shows how fundamental is their feeling of responsibility for the souls of the dead. On All Saints' Day all of Brittany leaves a meal ready on the table and lights in the room, that the departed ones may have food and comfort on this one night in the year when they can return to the scenes of their former lives.

The story goes that Yann Postik did not observe this custom, nor did he pray for souls in torment. All his life was spent in the careless pursuit of heartless pleasure. He laughed when his mother died and danced at the death of his wife, then alone and carefree he continued to give himself to worldly joys.

All Saints' Day came; he passed it in ribald song, in drink and in dancing, then night having long since fallen, he started for his home with a storm gathering in the distance. The way was long and when he reached a fork he took the shorter, haunted road without a thought that the other was guarded by a shrine. He passed a house; the weathervane upon it turned in the wind and cried: "Go back, Yann, go back!" but he went on. He came to a stream which murmured: "Do not go forward!" but he went. He came to an oak which whispered: "Stay, Yann, stay!" but he went on.

Midnight came and as he whistled and sang the noise of wheels came to his ears, mingled with the roar of thunder. There came a cart draped in black and driven by the figure of Death. Yann asked what brought him so late upon the road and Death replied: "I have come for the dead who yet speaks and moves. I have come for Yann Postik." Yann laughed and went on until he saw two young girls in white, spreading linen upon the grass. He asked what they did so far abroad and so late at night and they answered: "We wash, we dry and we sew. We are making the winding sheet for one who lives and moves, for Yann Postik."

Again Yann laughed and went on, and as the storm broke he heard the noise of "Those Who Wash by Night" beating clothes in the pool. They sang as they washed, an eerie song, and when they perceived him they ran to him and begged him to help them dry the linen by turning it with them. He accepted scornfully, knowing that if he turned it in the same direction as they did their power could not touch him. Other phantoms gathered about, pressing close to him. He recognized his wife, his mother, relatives and friends who wailed at him wearily, drearily: "A thousand curses on him who forgets the dead, a thousand curses on him who forgets his prayers, a thousand curses on him who lets his nearest suffer in hell."

He was frightened and confused. He turned the linen in the opposite direction and fell dead, while the spirits shrieked and wailed to the accompaniment of the storm.

POITIERS

SITUATED on a high ridge, Poitiers overlooks the fertile plains on either side in which ripen the famous Poitou peaches so deep in color and so rich in flavor. The air was cool and clear when we arrived, after a most destructive thunder storm which had raged for hours and had left the country windswept but wet and the people considerably refreshed. The whole atmosphere of the town was dignified, scholarly and devout; we felt we were among a people whose entire being was centered in their intellectual and family life and in the expression of their religious beliefs. It is an ecclesiastical as well as a university city and it offers the student a veritable feast of Romanesque architecture in all its different aspects and adaptations, containing more fine examples of this style perhaps than any other French city.

At first the place seems rather a modern one and then, as one knows it better, it proves itself to be a city of shy reserves and unexpected beauties — like its inhabitants. As we picked a precarious way along a narrow, steep street lined by busy shops, it was a pleasant surprise to raise our eyes and find over our heads two magnificent gargoyles jutting out from the roof line of an exquisite gable with Renaissance carvings. A high, severe wall permitted us just a glimpse of a fine Jesuit chapel, while a boys' school of uninteresting exterior contained a court on one wall of which were sixteenth century medallions and a Gothic door. One of the most ancient relics of this part of France is a prehistoric dolmen, three vertical stones supporting a horizontal table found (of all places!) in a kitchen garden on the hill on the far side of the little river Clain. It is certainly a city of contrasts.

Local pride says that this eastern hill is the most ancient section of all and shows marks of the sea in the rocks of its foundation, a sure proof — according to the archæologist — of its having once been seashore or actually submerged. The dolmen is of unquestioned antiquity and the nearby Hypogeum, with its funeral chapel of the seventh century, is also authentic. Only a fragment of this most interesting building remains, some steps with delicate Merovingian carving, part of the walls and many stone tombs of the early Christian martyrs for whose burial it was erected. It was discovered and excavated some fifty years ago, so perhaps greater treasures lie there awaiting the light.

One bit of the old Roman arena can still be seen in the heart of the city. This was the largest in all Gaul and was only destroyed a few years ago when the zest for modern building incorporated it into new houses or used its massive stones for the construction of still others.

The most venerable building still standing is the Temple or Baptistery of St. Jean, the oldest Christian edifice in France. Built in the fourth century, part of its original north wall and the central baptismal font still exist. Other parts date as late as the eighth century and the entrance is, by comparison, very new, having only been constructed a thousand years ago. It is a very impressive thing to see and quite different from any other church we know. Unfortunately, as so often happens in a city of such antiquity, the level of the streets is now considerably higher in most parts than it was when the oldest structures were built. Statistics show an average rise of one foot every hundred years, I believe, so the old buildings seem sunken, built as they were on the original level while the modern streets encircling them are often as much as fifteen feet higher. A good view of the Temple is difficult to obtain as, because of its greater age and smaller area, it rises unobtrusively from its moat-like enclosure and consequently only a near observation discloses the real beauty of its primitive structure. In shape it is slightly cruciform, the main part of it square, with a rectangular entrance, and with small, domed chapels on the other three sides. The eastern one of these contained the altar, the others were used, one as a disrobing, the other as a robing room for the people who for many years were baptized by immersion in the deep central font. The walls were built of an ancient type of brick with interesting carvings under the eaves. The building is now used as a small museum and contains some tombs beautifully carved, the small baptismal basin which later superseded the use of the larger one and a marble stone, once the sacrificial slab of pagan times, later adorned with crosses and used as a Christian altar.

The cathedral of St. Pierre is another building depressed below the level of its surroundings, and it suffers especially from this because of the great and disproportionate width of its façade, a fact which makes it seem even less high than it really is. The plan of it is simple and uncompromising to a degree, one tremendous rectangle with short transepts; no curved apse, no radiating chapels, nothing to break the singleness of design. The exterior does not gain by this elimination of extraneous structure. The west façade, five steps below

[82]

the street level and with a small, uninteresting paved court, is so much too wide that with its out-jutting square, low towers, to which the spires were never added, it gives the impression of being hunched down uncomfortably between high shoulders. The portals are very fine, the central one of the Last Judgment being especially full of motion and feeling. The lower line of sculpture, where the dead are recklessly casting the coverings of their tombs aside, had for me a particularly dramatic appeal.

The north and south walls are long, high and lacking in interest, and the eastern one is very out of the ordinary in its complete lack of decoration or central motive. I have studied it and I have thought about it but I cannot yet reconcile myself to a high, flat apse. Seen from the street which runs along it, it suggests almost a prison, or better yet a fortress, with its few windows high above one's head and below them a great stretch of blank wall. This latter aspect is perhaps accentuated by the cannon marks still visible in the sturdy masonry, made by zealous "sans culottes" when they fired up the nearby street upon this symbol and house of ecclesiastical power. I think this end of the church must have been intended to be seen from afar. When we later crossed the river and drove, first up and then down the winding avenue which leads to the Gilded Virgin of the opposite hill, I almost reversed my first unfavorable impression of it. From there, with the nearby houses blotting out the featureless lower portion and with the upper wall and its windows rising clear and majestic over everything, it had a certain grandeur of size and setting. But even so, I would take in preference the simplest apse of conventional shape.

This rectangular plan greatly enhances the feeling of size in an already large interior. Save for a very few, I have seldom been in a cathedral which seemed so overwhelmingly enormous. This is due partly to the aisles, which are almost as wide as the central nave, and partly to the fact that no curved line at the eastern end breaks into the perspective. Except for this quality of size there is little of note in the interior; some small but interesting sculptures on the spandrels of the curved backs of the choir stalls, some carved brackets under the mouldings of the walls and magnificent sixteenth century windows to relieve the coldness. It seemed a white, barren church, rather unloved and unloving.

St. Hilaire, on the other hand, is a distinct contrast. This great Romanesque structure, begun in the fourth century, was rebuilt four times. It was sacked by the Visigoths in the fifth, by the Saracens in the eighth and the

Normans in the ninth; the eastern end and part of the tower date from its fourth rebuilding in the eleventh century. As I read and heard of the Saracen aggression it was interesting to speculate on what the appearance of this church might have been if Poitiers had gone down under their invasion instead of turning the tide. Here, under Charles Martel in 732, that great oriental horde which had swept relentlessly across the helpless country from Spain was stopped, then turned, and finally driven back again beyond the Pyrenees. If they had not been checked here, where would they have stopped, if at all? France, perhaps Europe, might have gone down under their ruthless, calculated onslaught and if that had happened no power on earth could have dislodged them. The world would now be Mohammedan and the great monuments Moorish.

But to go back to St. Hilaire. After its many vicissitudes it was finally sold at the time of the Revolution to a private individual who began demolishing it and selling the stone for building materials. Luckily, before the building was completely destroyed it was bought back by the Church and the nave rebuilt by a bishop of Poitiers at the end of the nineteenth century. This part is still unfinished and looks oddly new beside the great antiquity of the rest, but the original plan seems to have been faithfully adhered to and the rough blocks of stone which crown the modern shafts are to be carved and decorated when — or if — sufficient money is raised. The design of the interior is most interesting and unusual. I believe the cathedral of Le Puy is the only one which resembles it. The style is pure Romanesque, there are domes above the nave with curious shell-like vaulting in the corners which make the transition cleverly from the square of the base. Between the nave and lateral aisles is a double row of columns, joined by very small round arches, making a five aisled church and so increasing the number of arches that the curve of them is seen from every possible angle and in every possible perspective. It is really a very lovely effect. The altar is raised considerably above the nave and the shrine of the saint beneath is several steps below it. In fact this eastern end has four different elevations, with chapels on almost every one. The columns here retain traces of their original color and the capitals are elaborately carved in varying designs. There is a distinctly Byzantine feeling in much of the sculpture and in all of the painting, while in some capitals the Egyptian influence is quite marked, notably in those with a collarette of leaves above the neck of the shaft. Kept in the sacristy and in the base of the tower are some capitals even more elaborate than any in the church itself. The tower is a fifteenth century

POITIERS
CHURCH OF STE. RADEGONDE
Size of the original pencil drawing, 12⅝ inches by 5¾ inches

addition and was built in, and up through, the northern transept. Fortunately they left the original decoration, so that from a precarious foothold at the top of the worn spiral stair we had tantalizing views of carved brackets and yet more capitals.

Notre Dame la Petite, called so to distinguish it from its nearby neighbor Notre Dame la Grande, is still pathetically lovely in spite of its mutilated condition. Made into a fish market at the time of the Revolution, and with its whole upper structure lowered to a monotonous, even line, it is now part of the Palais de Justice which is another of the many surprising and beautiful buildings of this ever astonishing town. The latter edifice boasts a Salle des Pas Perdus worthy to be compared with any, of which one wall dates from the twelfth, one from the thirteenth, and one from the fourteenth century. The fourth is partially covered by a gigantic fireplace, the three flues from which rise on the exterior and cover quite a little of the glass of the great windows, with stone Gothic tracery, which complete this end. Yet in spite of these obstructions, the great hall is adequately lighted for its entire length of fifty meters. From the outside it looks as if it were a wall of solid masonry, yet so cleverly are the flues and buttresses built that they catch and reflect into the interior a greater quantity of light than the same area of free glass could give.

It was in this room that Jacques Cœur underwent his ordeal after his so-called trial — a judicial farce, a grim joke seldom equaled for dishonesty and ingratitude. They call these great waiting rooms "Halls of Lost Steps" because the advocates pace back and forth in them waiting for their cases to be called, while justice tarries. The "lost steps" of Jacques Cœur haunt this Salle at Poitiers, echoing to his lost fortune, his lost freedom and his lost faith in the honor of a king.

Beyond the great wall, thirty feet thick, is the tower where the archives of Paris were stored when that city was threatened in 1917. This room is filled with memories of Jeanne d'Arc. In 1429 this peasant girl followed Charles VII (then the Dauphin) to Chinon to tell him of her vision and to beg for his support of her claim. She was treated first as an adventuress, then as a fool. When after countless rebuffs she finally obtained the interview for which she had pleaded, she succeeded in convincing the king and his advisors of her sincerity, but not of her sanity. Poitiers, the one university city of that time, was the obvious place in which to test her mental health and here the doubting monarch sent her. For four long weeks she lived in the little Hotel de la Rose, the site of which is now known only by a marble slab, and daily in this tower room the learned professors and doctors of the day questioned her and endeavored in ingenious ways to trap her into some damaging admission. All in vain: they finally pronounced her sane and Charles came to Poitiers and was acclaimed king in this same room. The proclamation was then solemnized at the Cathedral of St. Pierre and later he was consecrated at Rheims. It was from Poitiers that Jeanne d'Arc started forth with her adored sovereign and his army, first for Chinon, then for Orléans and her great triumph.

A modern window in Notre Dame la Grande shows this scene of her mental judging. In style and period it is out of place, but one forgives those faults because it commemorates and causes to relive again for us such a stirring page of history.

Of all the churches of Poitiers this one of Notre Dame la Grande is the most beautiful. Both the exterior and interior of this extraordinary building are of the purest Romanesque style. The western façade is a thing of unimaginable loveliness. It is such a mass of delicate sculpture that not a single part remains undecorated, yet there is no feeling of crowding nor lack of central interest. The building is rather long and narrow, with no aisles, and the side walls are bare of ornament; all the loving wealth of detail has been concentrated on the one elevation. Carved doors and chiseled arches, bands of sculpture and flat surfaces covered with a network of light fish-scale pattern, succeed each other in brilliant and bewitching beauty. Above the crossing is a most interesting tower, the transition from the hexagonal form of the lower part to the circular one of the upper being cleverly designed. It is covered, as are the small turrets on either side of the main façade, with triangular stones set point up so that the surface suggests almost that of a pineapple. This is very reminiscent of some of the roofings of Perigord.

The interior is as pure in type as the exterior, the columns are polychrome, faded and streaked to yet lovelier shades, and the capitals are elaborately carved and gilded. But no matter what the beauty of this, or of other parts might be, I always returned to a contemplation of the main façade where I marveled again and again over its wealth of detail.

Ste. Radegonde, which J. T. decided to draw, is largely Romanesque, with a fine tower and Gothic door. Here too the level of the ground is higher than that of the church, necessitating a forecourt, but in this case they have made rather a feature of it and it blends perfectly. In this court were held ecclesiastical law sessions when the power of the church was temporal as well as spiritual, and here the children now play ball and marbles and the old women sit about

with baskets of thin candles to burn before the shrine. For this is the very
sacred church of Poitiers and one to which the pious pilgrims still come to ask
and often to receive, if one may judge by the many offerings about the tomb.
Built in the eighth century and sacked, rebuilt again and yet again, only the
crypt and shrine under the high altar remain of the first church of ancient
times. A wide flight of stairs leads down into the darkness to the place where
rests the tomb of the saint, covered by tin points for candles which always are
burning in greater or fewer numbers. The aisles of the crypt radiate left and
right from the tomb but are separated from it by a massive wall. Here are
three little chapels, cold, uncared-for, unilluminated; all the warmth and color
and devotion are concentrated in the central chapel with the sacred relics.

Over the crypt the main altar is raised high above the rest of the church.
Its choir of painted Romanesque columns with carved and gilded capitals
glows with the warm, dark coloring of time and the aisleless nave is full of
somber dignity. At the right a little chapel with life-size figures commemorates
a miracle which happened nearby. Queen Radegonde, Christian wife of Clo-
taire, became at last unable to endure the pagan life and practices of her husband and his court. She left him and came to Poitiers where she founded a
convent and devoted her life to her religion and to good works. One day the
Christ appeared to her and, telling her of her approaching death and future
celestial glory, added that she was a precious jewel in His crown. He disappeared but afterwards there was found a footprint in the rock which has been
preserved and transferred to this little chapel. The devout supplicant places a
burning candle before this shrine and throws a coin through the protecting
grating. If the coin falls in the sacred imprint, he feels sure that his prayer will
be granted, if not, that it may be answered anyway. The little floor is strewn
thickly with these metal offerings and many flames burn hopefully there.

On our last day in Poitiers, which happened also to be the first of the
week's festival in memory of this saint, we went to Mass at Ste. Radegonde and
I carried from it a lasting and colorful memory. From our seats we could see
the high altar, its strange tones of ancient times glowing deeply in the changing
light; the priest in his vestment of rich green moved softly to and fro, and
beneath all this light and warmth and motion the little tapers, symbols of
man's need to believe, flickered brightly in the velvety blackness about the
tomb.

ANGERS

AS often happens, the town most heralded as the unique, wonderful and not-to-be-missed spot, proved a distinct disappointment. We had heard of Angers always. Its cathedral, its tapestries, its quaint old streets and its feudal castle had all been extolled to the skies, until we felt it a very Promised Land and were all eager anticipation as we approached it. Our first view was of the castle, ancient stronghold of the Dukes of Anjou, then prison, now a military post with tin-roofed barracks inside the walls and rows of gleaming muskets stacked in the ancient chapel. The walk around the ramparts is fine, with views over the rolling countryside, and the seventeen towers are massive and strong in spite of the lapse of years. One misses their one-time height, for in 1589 Richelieu ordered them all lowered, out of jealousy towards the house of Anjou which offered the nearest competitor to his king. But surely this was an empty gesture of arrogant power, those extra feet of height at that period could not have meant much added strength, while the succeeding generations have lost the beauty of them. The castle, though larger than that of the Brittany Dukes at Nantes, is much less varied and is not to be compared with it for beauty.

Built on a hill, the streets of Angers are steep and narrow and turn with the contours of the ground. Here and there an old house leans out over the street, or a steep gable in a high-pitched roof serves as a reminder of mediaeval times, but these are rather rare. Most of the buildings are uninteresting and modern, uniformly roofed with the gray slate of this section. Behind the cathedral, quite the loveliest old house holds dignified sway upon its corner. Save for the modern windows of the first floor shop, it offers an untouched example of the best of the type. It is corbeled out three times, but not too far. Its timber work is stained a deep rich red and is carved with great variety and subtlety. One sees Adam and Eve and the fated apple tree, a swan with its young, a grinning grotesque figure or a charming head. An inner staircase is contained in an engaged tower, carried up for two floors and rich with sculptured details. Built of honest material and by honest labor on ample, solid lines, it was meant to withstand the years and well has it fulfilled its purpose.

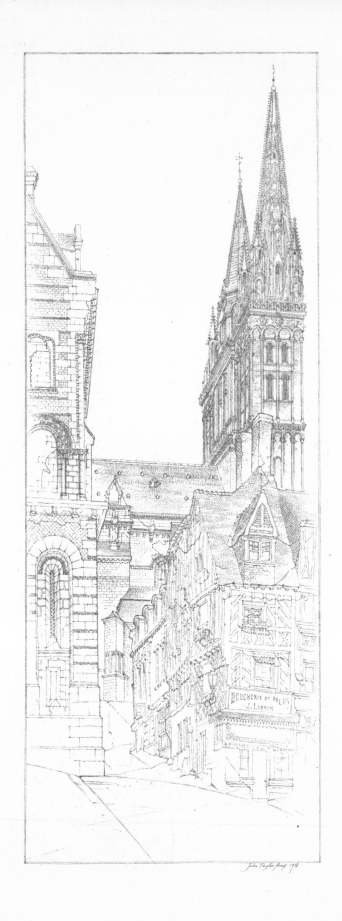

John Taylor Arms 1938

So far as eye can see, it is good for as many centuries more, and long may it stand as a bit of intrinsic beauty and a memorial of other times.

This was altogether satisfactory, but the cathedral was a bitter disappointment. It is so reconstructed, so restored, so jumbled and crowded by other buildings, that it is only possible to see it from two points. One from a side street reveals the best line of the towers, with a Renaissance building in the foreground as a charming foil, the other from the foot of the Montée St. Maurice shows a magnificent situation but too much of the curious and far from pleasing western façade. This "montée," which is neither stairs nor street but a compromise between the two, rises sharply up the hillside to the terrace upon which the cathedral is built. The first and most vivid impression is of the narrow, rather top-heavy spires, joined for almost their entire height by a third structure which starts out bravely to be a tower and ends up as a sort of hexagonal lantern, most distressingly ugly in itself and quite destroying all beauty or upward line of the other two. The result is an unfortunate illusion that everything above the line of the roof has only two dimensions — height and width — but that depth is lacking. It is a sort of monumental false front, one might say. This is particularly to be regretted as the north tower is quite lovely, with simple vertical lines, and the south one, though less interesting, is fine in mass. They are, however, disfigured by the central structure. The portal is good but woefully inadequate, overwhelmed as it is by the frieze of gigantic figures above it and unsupported by other entrances on either side. The low lateral chapels — obviously later and quite inconsistent additions — are too small and unimportant to help the solidity of the base, and the general effect is of a long, thin rectangle on a too small foundation. In consequence, the top appears considerably wider than the bottom.

The interior lacks interest except for the tapestries which hang from the gallery on each side of the nave. These are scenes from the Apocalypse and date from the fifteenth century in some cases, whereas the first Gobelins were made in the seventeenth. Even more beautiful examples are in the one-time Episcopal Palace adjoining. Here, hung about the walls of the great banqueting hall, are some of the most extraordinary works of art that the mind and hand of man have brought into being. Fabricated all those centuries ago and for long years so absolutely neglected that in the nineteenth century they were sold with out-of-date furniture for rags, they are still brilliant and almost intact. What was the secret that has kept the tones so rich and varied and — more surprising still — uneaten by the ever present moth? Even more astonishing than the physical marvel of their endurance is the maturity of thought and conception which guided their making. We smiled over the ingenuous representation of a town, its houses tottering and falling from the shock of an earthquake, but there is nothing naïve or simple in the character portrayal evinced in most of the figures. These are individuals, faithfully depicted in their physical attributes even to such homely things as a disfiguring mole or a double chin, but with subtly suggested personalities besides. One is torn between admiration for the cunning which represents a negro's arm seen through his thin sleeve or shows the contrast between a rich brocaded robe and one of gleaming velvet, and the mental power which could so express the intense spirituality of the face of St. John as well as the gross vulgarity of that of the equestrian demon.

These tapestries alone would make a pilgrimage to Angers worth any effort, but only these would justify the trip in my opinion. Why then the tremendous enthusiasm for this rather uninspiring place? Can it be that here one is in the heart of the great vine-growing center of Anjou and that its famous wines so bias opinion that even the uninteresting cathedral is seen through rose-colored spectacles? I wonder.

LIMOGES

LIMOGES has rain and possibly snow, though the latter must be infrequent in the city's inland, temperate situation. But in my memory it is always sunny there. I see it with a pall of heavy smoke from the factory chimneys thick over the low-lying sections, while the sky arching over it is of that clear metallic blue which comes only with dry heat.

We had just left Poitiers, with its quality of other days and its Sabbath stillness, and the plunge into this commercial city came with a shock of contrast. It was a place of sirens, of clanging trams and of whistling trains and everywhere there was an air of businesslike confusion. The inhabitants of the two cities were as dissimilar. Those of Poitiers had been tranquil, contented and all apparently in comfortable circumstances, but those of Limoges were hurried and anxious, and poverty was often apparent. Blocks of houses were being torn down. On their remaining walls scarred papers and once welcoming fireplaces could be seen. Efficient white buildings, wholly lacking in beauty, were being constructed in their stead and the air was thick with plaster dust, while workmen abounded.

Stores hung out eager signs with which to catch the attention of the passer-by and competition was keen even to the point of bitter personal remarks. For the first and only time in France I heard (not once but many times) a shopkeeper say that I might find a similar article " chez mon confrère" but that it would be more expensive or poor in quality. Ill-will did not prompt the remark, but the desperate struggle for a bare existence which cannot count the cost to others. People were pleasant and courteous but the typical Latin gaiety was conspicuously absent. We felt them sad and grim, haunted by the demon of industrialism — a malignant power which crushes individualism and destroys human souls.

Years of routine work have taken from these inhabitants of Limoges the warlike spirit inculcated in them by their first saint. St. Martial is called the Apostle of Limousin and his story goes back to the very beginnings of Christianity. He is said to have been a friend of St. Amadour, to have dedicated the chapel at Rocamadour and to have been one of the first pilgrims to that shrine. Another legend tells of his founding the original church in Limoges. On the high hill above the river was a much venerated temple to Jupiter which was anathema to this well-named saint. One fine day he and his followers entered the pagan precincts, destroyed the images and claimed the temple by right of might, rededicating it to St. Stephen. The legend is not authenticated, though during the recent excavations necessitated by the building of the eastern portion of the cathedral nave, fragments of sculpture and walls of great antiquity were unearthed. They do not guarantee the truth of the story but they do help to substantiate it.

After the temple, a Romanesque basilica was erected of which only the tower remains, that beautiful tower which is said to have been the model and the inspiration for all the similar structures in Limousin. It stands solidly upon its oblong foundation, a little apart from the cathedral. The upper stories are octagonal but set so that their angles project from the sides of the square base beneath them. The corners have rounded buttresses which become free, slender turrets at the uppermost tier and the simple windows have the characteristic louvers of this section. The spire no longer exists, but even without it the tower is very high and very fine. It is dignified and a little aloof, perhaps even a trifle severe, as are the people under its surveillance.

Save for this feature and some of the foundations, the cathedral is Gothic. The old Romanesque basilica was replaced by the newer style and a part of the nave was finished in the fifteenth century. Work stopped then, only to be resumed and completed a hundred years ago when the nave was carried out to the designed length and joined to the belfry by a form of narthex or porch. This forced union of two dissimilar units is most unfortunate from the west side. From here one sees the strong, splendid tower in front of an abortive façade which is neither off to one side nor directly back of it. The deviation is too small to be right and too great to be inconspicuous, it is merely disturbing.

The rest of the exterior is fine. Seen from the old bridges which cross the Vienne, or from the other side of the river, the church piles up magnificently above the houses beneath it. The apse is high and has a springing freedom about it greatly accentuated by the ridge on which it is built and the sudden falling away of the hill beyond. A nearer view reveals transepts of great delicacy, an unexpected quality in this otherwise simple and rather severe building. They are both very short, the northern one especially so. It extends so little beyond the line of the nave that we felt it must have been used merely as an excuse for so much lovely ornamentation.

The interior gives, first and last, an impression of vastness. This must be

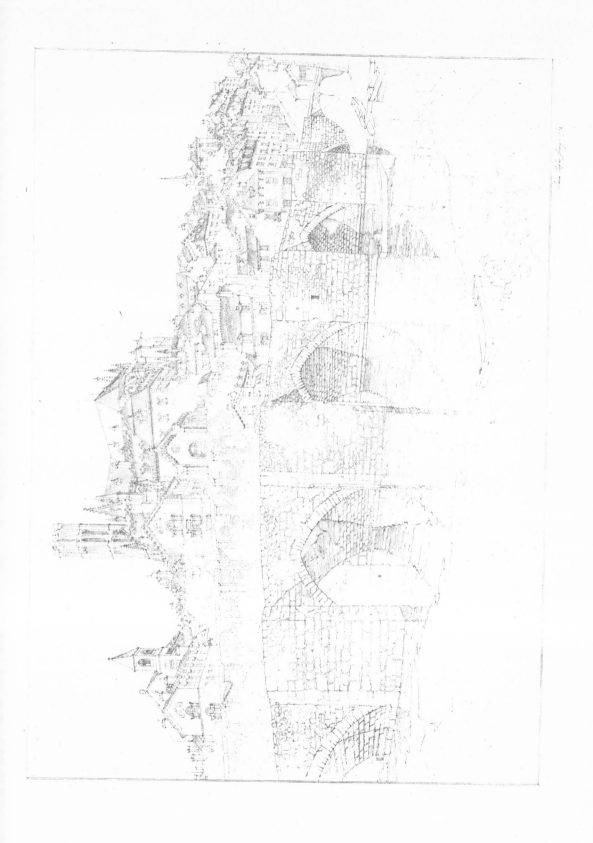

felt and said, I feel sure, by everyone who enters it, for I think I have never seen a building in which one quality so predominates. We entered through the base of the old belfry, feeling somehow as if it were a back door, so unimportant and inconspicuous is it as a portal. We passed through the connecting porch and came out under the carved Renaissance Rood Loft into the immense nave. It seemed as if we had dropped suddenly into limitless space, it was so huge, so overwhelmingly immense.

It is interesting that man cannot seem to comprehend size until it becomes circumscribed. We walk about with the infinite sky above us, feeling quite contented and comfortable until we climb a precipitous mountain or enter a mighty building. Then only, either by the knowledge of the heights we have scaled or by the walls greater than those to which our eyes are accustomed, do we grasp a little of the meaning of space. Our human vision is limited to that which we can measure by some little yardstick of personal experience.

So the cathedral of St. Étienne filled us with awe and wonder by its suggestion of size. It is big, and seems even more so because of the clever widening of the apsidal chapels and the delicate columns which rise to such unbelievable heights. There are details of interest and some lovely glass of brilliant tones. The old part of the nave has mellowed to a warm, brownish gray but the newer portion is still too pale for unity; the grime and soot of antiquity have not yet completed their appointed mission. It is hard, however, to concentrate on other things; one wants to give oneself up to space, to lose oneself in the feeling of immensity which this cathedral engenders.

St. Pierre is in the busy, commercial part of the city. It was intended for a five aisled church and is one essentially, though the design is not completely carried through. Why it was not constructed far enough to the south to permit of this, or if the contours of the earth necessitated its being placed exactly where it is, why the line of the street was not changed, remains a mystery. At the eastern end the five aisles are distinct and unimpeded, the southernmost one lightly divided by low grilles to form lateral chapels, but the northern wall slants at such an angle along the street that the outermost aisle has completely disappeared by the time it reaches the western end. The columns are round and strong, with capitals of sculptured leaves, and there are so many of them that one feels in a forest of sturdy trees.

The belfry of St. Pierre and that of St. Michel des Lions both resemble that of the cathedral, though the one of St. Michel has an odd, ball-shaped termination of fretted copper which is curious but hardly in keeping with its dignity. It gets its name from two quite indistinguishable beasts at the southern entrance. Once bravely sculptured, of the gray granite like stone of the country, they have been worn and rubbed away until — like the children of the too-cleanly Dutch mother — their features have been completely washed from their faces. Two dimples above and one below are all that remain to show that here was once a pair of eyes and there a fierce and open mouth.

The church they guard is so much in the center of things, so engulfed by the crowding city, that it is difficult to find. I must have walked completely around it before I finally discovered it at the end of a little street. I went in past the lions and under the belfry, with no thought but that this was the main portal, and then I had the curious illusion of being in a church built sideways, with the width of the building greater than that of its length. Everything conspired to increase the effect. Opposite to me, in what I realized later was the north wall, were two simple chapels, one of which contained the most sacred statue and towards which all the chairs were turned and the prayers of the kneeling figures directed. It took me a little time to get my proper orientation and to realize that I had come through a side door into a church whose plan is simplicity itself, that of a long, narrow rectangle. There is no apse and the eastern, like the western wall, is flat and with similar windows of highly colored glass. Not even a variation in level marks it as the spot which usually contains the sanctuary, only an inconspicuous main altar distinguishes it from the other end.

The great beauty is the vaulting. The body of the church is divided into a central and two side aisles by the means of very slender clustered columns. But the usual connecting arches and units of separate vaulting are absent; instead, the ribs of the groining spring from each column in four directions, forming a single roof. This is similar to the treatment we have found in several Salles des Gardes, where a central pillar holds all the vaulting or where there are two rows of columns. The interior gains greatly in an effect of architectural lightness, but it loses sadly in structural strength. Certain of the shafts looked alarmingly out of line, though the safety of the building has, I believe, been recently guaranteed by a board of Parisian architects.

One evening we walked up the Rue de la Boucherie, that well-known street of which the modern Limousin is secretly ashamed. He tells you proudly that, with new butcher shops and the fine market, this street is no longer as prosperous or important as it used to be and that soon perhaps it will disappear

altogether. If it does, then I am glad the fates led us here before that anticipated day.

Limoges was always a city of " confrèries," the members of which were
bound together against all other organizations. Prominent among them was
the association of butchers, who still cling to old houses and old traditions
as well as to their old trade. This narrow street is their very own, a closed
circle, practically a family affair, for they have intermarried for many years.
They say that when Henry IV came to Limoges the townspeople went to meet
him as a guard of honor and preceded him into the city. They marched by
guilds with the butchers in the rear, who, realizing that they of all others were
nearest to the king, arrogated to themselves this post of honor in all subsequent royal entries. This led to rivalry and much unpleasant feeling but the
stalwart meat-men carried the day and welcomed the honored visitor in a body.
In 1845 the city government refused them the privilege, so they left secretly
on horseback to meet the Duke and Duchess of Nemours in the country.
These, pleased by the attention, enjoyed their escort back to town, to the mortification of the unsuspecting officials.

Many of the butchers' descendants live in this street named for their
trade. It is short and very narrow, every house in it is old, with many jutting
gables. In the lower part of each is a shop for meat or fish and the odor which
emanates from them and from the very pavement exceeds even its reputation.
It inclines one strongly to a vegetarian diet for some time afterwards.

At an angle of the street stands the little chapel dedicated to St. Aurelian,
successor to St. Martial, a tiny building no higher than the surrounding houses.
Simple, primitive, ancient, it has been the butchers' church since earliest times
and to them it is especially dear, especially venerated. It is of deep-toned
stone, with a gray slate roof. The quaint little belfry slants upward in a more
or less conventional line, then suddenly changes its direction and blossoms out
into a curious pinnacle rather like an inverted lily.

Before the shrine outside the church a light burns every night, once oil,
now gas, later electricity perhaps. Customs vary, places change, methods of
illuminating improve, but the little light always burns.

PÉRIGUEUX

I AM not one of those who bewail all restoration, whether good, bad, or indifferent. The purist who raises up his voice in indignant protest against all forms of repair with his battle cry of "Better a crumbling ruin than a restored building however good" is, to my way of thinking, a little narrow in his point of view. Granted that to many people who have made an intensive study of history, architecture or literature, and who have had the opportunity of wide travel, a vine covered ruin may be most significant with the walls half gone and with only slight traces left of the one-time banqueting hall or postern gates, or whatever it may be. To such people these crumbling fragments are more vision-provoking than the finest feudal castle carefully rebuilt. So the cartoon of a master is of as great value to an artist as the finished work, and vastly more so than the same canvas repainted by no matter what careful, loving hands. To his trained eye the first drawing is spontaneous and real, the retouched painting almost a reproduction. But for the many people who have not had time, opportunity or inclination for highly specialized training, an intelligent restoration is of incomparable value. There the thing is before their eyes, not to be guessed at or imagined — often erroneously — but complete and historically accurate. Conscientious restoration, which remains absolutely faithful to its model, seems to me to have an increasingly important place in our civilization and in our appreciation of ancient beauty as time and the damage wrought by the years, the elements and that ever present danger of fire, take increasing toll of the historic monuments still remaining to us.

On the other hand, when I see a magnificent cathedral like that of St. Front at Périgueux rebuilt, re-made out of almost all semblance of its one-time beautiful self, I become as bitter as the fanatics themselves. It is still so fine, particularly in its great piled-up exterior with the almost oriental domes and turrets, that one only realizes what has been irreparably lost by comparing the present building with pictures of the original made nearly a hundred years ago. In them one feels the structural changes which time and the needs of an ever growing congregation had brought about in the first building. To the nucleus which had once proved adequate, chapels and extensions had been added from time to time until a mass of structure and superstructure rose in heterogeneous

PÉRIGUEUX
A TOWER OF ST. FRONT
Size of the original etching, $11\frac{7}{8}$ inches by $5\frac{1}{2}$ inches

PÉRIGUEUX
A TOWER OF ST. FRONT
Size of the original etching, $11\frac{7}{8}$ inches by $5\frac{1}{2}$ inches

John Taylor Arms · 1928

but pleasing confusion. It may have been shabby, it certainly lacked the unity of the present church, but it must have had a more lovable and a more sympathetic personality than the one we feel to-day. It puts me in mind of the old, old medical joke, that the operation was perfectly successful but unfortunately the patient died. The architects of the nineteenth century, who so painstakingly rebuilt their cathedral, hoped by standardizing it, by drawing it together in singleness of style, to make a whole so beautiful and so pure that all the world would marvel, but they succeeded instead in taking sadly from its character.

The present exterior is so fine that this tirade may seem exaggerated. I, personally, regret the old building of jumbled roofs, though I can see a certain justification for their destruction; but in the interior I see no alleviation whatsoever. It is built in the form of a Greek cross, over the center of which is a high wide dome and over each arm a smaller one. The square central piers are massive Romanesque affairs pierced through all four sides by high, slender openings with narrow arches. This multiplication of the arched motive seems to me the only unusual and interesting note. It lends a quality of unexpectedness to an interior otherwise as featureless, as cold and as unsympathetic as a swimming tank. The apse inclines strongly to the north, which in this building of mechanical perfection must have been deliberately planned, it could not have been the result of an accident. One can almost hear the anxious architects discussing the matter and weighing the pros and cons of this feature. Chance, or the beautiful thought of the bent head of Christ as He hung dead upon the Cross, had caused that deviation from the straight line of the nave in so many of the historic churches. Should they keep to the cold precision of their calculated plans or should they follow tradition? They chose wrongly, for in this building of curves in which one feels the unswerving compass, of unvarying vertical and horizontal lines, the inclined apse is almost grotesque. Blind arcading in the transepts and incongruous Corinthian capitals in the choir and chapels are the only decorations, save for the simplest of Romanesque mouldings.

Two incidents happened which seemed to me significant of this lack of a lovable personality in the church. Having walked about and studied mass and detail until my head was turning both physically and mentally, I sank down upon a chair in a state of exhaustion. The great basilica was almost empty, a slammed door reverberated loudly, distant and unlowered voices from the loft where a screen was being painted to simulate organ pipes echoed back from the white, cold domes, and the departing worshipers betook themselves in the direction of their noonday meal with the characteristic squeaking of their French shoes unpleasantly accentuated. An old lady near me seemed my only companion in that great interior of resounding spaciousness. She presently finished her prayer, sat back and, lifting her market bag to her knees, drew forth from that capacious receptacle her morning's purchases; a bunch of parsley, three ruddy tomatoes, a handful of small onions and a fine green head of lettuce. She surveyed them critically one by one, then, seeming satisfied with their appearance, she put them back, and shaking her black skirts free of leaves and dirt she rose and left me to my solitary contemplation.

Some time later I became conscious that I was no longer alone by hearing a portentous throat-clearing going on near me. So long and so violently did it continue that I finally lifted a solicitous gaze in the direction of the sound. There was an old gentleman, supposedly deep in his devotions. As I observed him, anxiously wondering what first-aid measures might help him in his apparently violent seizure, he looked me squarely in the eye with an expression of extreme coyness and winked!

I can hardly imagine either episode happening in a church where the feeling of sanctity prevails, in Notre Dame de Paris or its name sister of Chartres, for example. Even the importunate beggars of the dirty, degenerate type who hung about the doors of St. Front were different from the usual single patient figure who merely sits pathetically and whose mute presence is more touching — and more efficacious — than any long whine of misery. The busy modern streets were empty in the noonday hour, the church seemed stranded from its people, as if the tide of religious need had ebbed away.

A sign, lettered in uncompromising clearness "This way to the old town," guided our footsteps a bit resentfully in that direction. We much prefer to do our exploring and discovering on our own account. But in spite of the sign, within a distance of a few yards we found ourselves in the old narrow streets of an ancient city. The section was not large but so perfect, so unspoiled that we felt ourselves transported back three or four centuries into a life which we had heretofore known only by hearsay. Gables and half-timber work abounded, quaint steps ascended in unexpected spots, while carved doorways and massive wooden doors, nail-studded, became such a common occurrence that ultimately we omitted even mentioning them. And the people of this section had an old-time courtesy and interest quite in keeping with their surroundings.

It was Sunday and the quarter was in restful holiday mood. Most of the inhabitants seemed to be on the streets, walking idly about, or pausing in conversational groups, or sunning themselves in the infrequent spots where the projecting roofs were far enough apart to permit the pale spring light to penetrate. The sketch book and camera therefore attracted more than the usual amount of attention and we soon had a following crowd of interested but respectful spectators. One man promptly constituted himself our special guide. By profession he was a barber, but he had the soul of a true artist and he led us from detail to detail with a subtle appreciation of each beauty. He naïvely confessed to a young brother " who also was an artist like Monsieur " and soon we noticed a bright-eyed boy in the group about us, carrying a large framed picture as inconspicuously as its obvious size would permit. It was the young brother with his maiden effort, an oil painting in which a certain ingenuousness vied with that sophistication in art to which all Frenchmen are born the natural heirs. It was a good canvas, too, I have seen worse in many exhibitions.

From many streets we could see the tower of St. Front, that curious tower which is the very essence of the architectural style of Périgord and yet is so individual as to be unmistakable. Superficially it looks as simple as the piled-up blocks of a child, a smaller cube placed upon a larger one beneath, but in the crowning motive, in the balance of the proportions, in the clever handling of the contrasts of flat surface and deep penetration brought about by the use of tiers of arched openings, it is a masterpiece of subtle, studied designing. The culminating turret is repeated in a miniature way on all the domes. They stand up sharply like pointing fingers, but in this larger one the curves are wider and more gracious, the angles less acute. On the roof which covers the square tower is built a round motive from which rises a circle of columns, infinitely slender and close set, and which in turn is completed by the cone so typical of Périgord. The curved slates which roof it, overlapping each other in perfect alignment, are spoken of as fish-scales and the name is certainly applicable, though the style suggested to me then, and has since as I have found it repeated on my various wanderings, a symmetrical pineapple done in stone.

This high-peaked cone and the airy colonnade beneath it are visible from every section of the town and come in time to seem its essence and guardian spirit. No longer aloof, it broods over the calm, contemplative streets of the ancient section and the hurrying, heedless ones of the newer portion, with its old-time, protecting love.

ANGOULÊME

SIMILAR to St. Front at Périgueux yet differing from it in many essential ways, St. Pierre at Angoulême comes to my mind always when I think of the other. Separated by only a short distance, having much the same historical, architectural and climatic background, they are similar enough to make their contrasts very significant. Both are near to Spain and their slated, cone-like turrets must have a Moorish ancestry, however remote, while their domed vaulting suggests the same source. There is a certain tropical quality in both which can only flourish in the warm suns of the south, and which would be so misplaced on the bleak northern coast that, if a similar church were built there, I feel sure that it would shortly cease to exist. Fancy worshiping under the white-tiled coldness of a Périgord vaulting while a snow storm raged and howled without! One's piety would shrivel into nothingness and one would seek a Gothic interior where brilliant windows and soft gray stone with deep-toned shadows would comfort the heart and would symbolize the warmth of religious belief.

Only people of a warm climate would build churches such as those of Angoulême and Périgueux. The exteriors are elaborate, the bands of Romanesque sculpture cast strongly bold shadows which are beautiful in their repeated pattern and can be enjoyed by people whose eyes are accustomed to the glare of a pitiless sun. But when the great portals close behind them as they enter for a time of worship, then comes the need for cool spaces where a minimum amount of color and ornament may rest their physical vision and so release their minds for inward contemplation. It is axiomatic that a change of occupation, however violent, is a rest and so this contrast here seems logical. In the north, to eyes accustomed to the suave contours and restful greens of those wide spreading fertile fields, the bright accents of highly colored windows and the complicated tracery of Gothic detail offer a mental stimulus which must have a vital place in religious fervor. Here visual relaxation is needed, the nearest approach to harmonious nothingness, in order that there may be physical and mental peace.

This may be a too personal theory but it seems to me possible, and Saint Pierre of Angoulême is a striking example of it. It is Romanesque, with a dis-

ANGOULÊME

THE CATHEDRAL OF ST. PIERRE

Size of the original etching, 6¼ inches by 11¼ inches

John Taylor Arms 1925

tinct dash of the Byzantine. The west façade is such a mass of sculpture that hardly one surface remains uncarved. It has been severely criticized, I know, yet I have always found it pleasing in a certain rhythmic quality and also because I have a prejudice in favor of carrying detail either a very little or a very long way; I like a wall severely plain with one deep portal, chiseled to a high degree, or I like the whole surface well covered by detail. To me the unpleasing façade is the one which carries its ornamentation too far and yet not far enough.

Abadie, whose restoration I regret at Périgueux, has here rebuilt a church which, partly because of its magnificent situation on the battlements of a narrow ridge high above the Charente, and partly because of the beautiful, unspoiled northern tower, remains with me as a poignant memory. This tower is the glory of Angoulême and one of the outstanding architectural treasures of France. Of the purest Romanesque style, it rises solidly square yet lightened by arcades of columns and round arches on each side of the slightly stepped-back stories. On the lowest of these there are only two openings on each face, sturdy looking in their simple massive line; on the next, three more delicately built; above that a triple motive subdivided by three slender columns; and crowning all a clustered arrangement of five small arches. The progression of scale is logical and so delicately graded from story to story that a result of great lightness is obtained.

The contrast is startling between the exterior, where turrets and tower, sculptured masses and deep shadowed portals, bring about a quality of cheerful energy, and the interior where cold severity reigns. The plan is cruciform, but instead of the vaulting which the straight line of the roof had led us to expect, the long aisleless nave is covered by a succession of wide, shallow domes, symmetrically perfect, white and cold. It is a chilling shock at first and it takes time to discern the real beauty of the whole. It is austere certainly, but not with the barren lack of sympathy which we felt in St. Front, it has instead more a feeling of reserve. There is a wealth of varied but unobtrusive Romanesque detail which warms the surface of the spandrels and of the vaulting without detracting from the unswerving quality of their lines.

I was struck, as I studied it, by the uncanny way in which a church so often takes on the characteristics and attributes of its patron saint. We name a child for the one we would have it resemble and more often than not our wish is granted. The apparent character or career may vary widely, but fundamentally there seems to be a certain similarity of mind processes as if a sympathetic bond held the two lives together. Is there a thought consciousness of that other person which tinges the whole nature of the younger one? And so this church of St. Pierre, dedicated to the most contradictory yet the most understandable of the Apostles, is a building of contrasts, of great beauties and of mistakes. Poor St. Peter, what sorrow his errors must have brought to his loving, devoted heart! He was capable of the greatest sacrifice, he bore his martyrdom with a fortitude remarkable even at that time, he was eager and zealous, wise and good, yet he was with it all so very human, impulsive, thoughtless and once deliberately wrong. The old writers say that all his days he wept ceaselessly over the remembrance of the night when he denied his Lord, and that the constant tears marked his cheeks with red lines of anguish. How glad he must have been to lay down his responsibilities and his tempestuous life at last. It is fitting that this church of Angoulême, and many others dedicated to him, should show, not alone the contrasts of his nature, but also the peace which came to him ultimately.

ROCAMADOUR

GRIM is the country of Auvergne; with forbidding hills, with cities of austere colors and contours and with a soil only productive of the sterner needs of life. Here one may look in vain for the pleasant valleys where cattle browse and grow sleek and fat, for the sunny slopes where grapes ripen to bursting sweetness or for the fields of wheat or oats rippling in the breeze. This is a harder land and as one's road leads upward from the comparative fertility of the country around Cahors to the uninhabited uplands of the Cévennes, one feels as if Doré himself must have had this country in mind when he cut some of his haunted and haunting wood blocks. The hills are naked and uncompromising in outline, between the boulders small flocks of sheep graze hurriedly with a hunger never satisfied, while a lone shepherd and his dog watch them silently. Everywhere great rocks are strewn haphazard as if some giants had thus thrown them about in aimless play.

We came through this aloof countryside one never-to-be-forgotten morning. The spirit of it had taken such a hold upon our imaginations that we were prepared for almost any uncanny manifestations. Home, the kind of people we knew and the safe, suave landscape we had so recently left seemed far away — things of another world. The only realities were the hills, the tumbled stones and the road that ascended steadily, inexorably. The valley narrowed and the great hills drew closer, still more narrow and more close until we found ourselves winding along the side of a cliff in a straightened, slender mountain gorge. A little green valley and the dry bed of a stream were below us. We turned and turned with the indentations of the hill and suddenly around one more bend we came upon Rocamadour, "the unbelievable town," the shrine of countless pilgrimages. It seems an integral part of the mountain side to which it clings so closely, and which in turn rises with such abrupt steepness that the little town appears to have only two dimensions, height and width. Depth has been almost eliminated. A closer view confirmed this first impression; we found the houses not above and behind each other but actually so nearly one upon the top of the one below as to increase, rather than decrease, this illusion. All the rooms are at the front, for the back wall of each house is built deep into the rock of the hillside. We found later that in order to begin the climb up the zigzag path which leads to the Calvary above, it was first necessary to go into our hotel by the front door, climb three flights of stairs and go out by the roof. From the windows of our rooms we looked down across the café on the other side of the street upon the terrace beyond, through the floor of which grew the top of a healthy tree whose roots struck into the hillside many feet below. Truly it is a life upon a ladder for man or growing thing.

One narrow street, a mere shelf in the rock, forms the town. It holds together the houses on either side as a slender thread holds heavy beads. And as in the one case the center ornament is the largest, the most precious of them all, so here also in the middle of the composition and built far up the mountain side, structure upon the top of still more ancient structure, rise the clustered buildings of the venerated shrine.

That which was a simple monastery in the early days of Christianity is now a complicated mass of masonry built into the rock and up the hillside. As the cult grew in importance and pilgrims came in increasing numbers, the original buildings became too small to take care of them. New chapels were added to fill their needs and finally a lodging place was built upon the summit to house some of the many who came from afar.

About midway up the hill is the Plateau of St. Michel, around which cluster various chapels, the supposed tomb of St. Amadour and the little church the fame of whose miracle-working statue of the Virgin made this perhaps the greatest pilgrimage spot of the twelfth century. Projecting from a nearby wall is the hilt of a sword, facsimile of the Durandal of Rollo, nephew of Charlemagne, placed there in memory of his pausing at Rocamadour on his way to Roncesvalles.

History, legend and story all vary as to the foundation of Rocamadour, though all are agreed that the name comes from Rock of Amadour, or Amateur. Who was he? Zacchaeus perhaps who, converted by Christ, became a devoted member of the household with an especial veneration for the Virgin. He is said to have come to France with Mary, Martha and Lazarus and to have withdrawn himself to this desolate region to finish his life in establishing a cult in her honor. Or perhaps that Amadour, the hermit of Bethlehem, who only asked peace and isolation from the world that he might worship the memory of the Virgin in undisturbed tranquillity. He performed such miracles by the aid of holy relics that solitude and he became strangers and he finally fled and sought refuge in central France. Or again another Amadour who, having made a pact with the devil, was taken by him to Egypt. There St. Paul, the Hermit,

ROCAMADOUR
ROCAMADOUR
Size of the original etching, 13⅞ inches by 10½ inches

Rocamadour 1926

John Taylor Arms 1927

released him from his wicked bond and he returned to France, founded a church to the Madonna and devoted his life to her cult.

Another legend says that St. Didier, Bishop of Auxerre, buried his mother Necterie beside the tombs of his predecessors St. Germain and St. Amadour. When the Saracens began sweeping across the country the holy relics were removed to a distant place for the sake of safety. There are many other versions, none of which bothered the devout pilgrims at all. This was their dearly loved, deeply venerated shrine, to which they came in their hour of desperate need. Many subsequently went their respective ways, their sins forgiven them or the boon they craved granted. Others returned home without a visible answer to their prayers but testifying to the divine help which, though it had refused the material favor, yet had granted them such abundant spiritual aid.

They came from near at hand, then as the fame spread of the miraculous Madonna which was said to have been carved by St. Amadour, they began coming from farther and farther off until foreign lands sent many pilgrims. The miracles extended even to those who had not yet reached the shrine. Records tell of a man set upon by robbers as he neared his goal. He implored the Virgin's help and his assailants' hands could not touch his gold nor their weapons injure him. Of the man who fell from a mountain side and reached the valley uninjured because he had thought to pray for help as he fell.

The finest stories are of the people to whom these pilgrimages meant a widening of their thought for others, not only a self-seeking quest, however justifiable. There was the Prince of Lorraine who, dismounting, put on his horse's back a sick woman and so brought her to the shrine. There he and his followers prayed for and with her until she was cured of her illness and went away. Then there was another cavalier, who rescued a woman half eaten by wolves and carried her to Rocamadour where health was restored to her. What with wolves and robbers and other accidents of travel, it was over a perilous way that they came, and it is no wonder that the saying grew that the Virgin, wishing to demonstrate her dominion over the hearts of men, had endowed with greatest power her shrine which was most inaccessible and most dangerous to reach.

The scenes in that chapel must have been strange and weird. Crippled beggars asked for alms at the door, the dying and very ill lay upon the floor, insane persons in clanking chains shrieked and groaned, people knelt in prayer beating their breasts and wailing their supplications or giving forth exultant cries as they felt their prayers were being answered.

The walls were hung with votive offerings; crutches, silver teeth to symbolize those miraculously grown, iron fetters, images in wax of resuscitated people or prison towers. These gifts poured in for years and pilgrims came in steady streams and then, who knows just how or why, the popularity of the shrine fell away, new ones superseded it and soon Rocamadour was left to its magnificent isolation.

We climbed the hill to the Calvary many times. We left by the roof of the hotel and went past a little garden consisting of one tiny marble bench and six potted plants which grew harmoniously beside the ridge pole, then on to the winding path which leads from one Station of the Cross to another. Each turn of the mounting way disclosed new beauties of view, trees shaded our going or open spaces gave us brilliant sunshine. The Calvary is at the summit, and nearby is the ancient château where the pilgrims were housed. From the roof of this building one can see the entire length of the valley of the Alzou, where the green ribbon of a river bed winds a narrow way between the precipitous mountains.

From there we descended past the Grottoes and various chapels, some in the living rock, others built out from it, all integral parts of a mighty whole. We came past the church and the plateau and down the two hundred and fifty-six steps up which, in September, pious pilgrims still go upon their knees. They are few in number now, but the long stone stair is peopled with a ghostly throng, kings and queens, cavaliers and their ladies, merchants, soldiers, sinners, saints and a myriad host whose remembered prayers whisper through the air on the summer winds.

LE PUY

IN Le Puy Nature has set herself to achieve the impossible. It is not credible that those high, thin needles of basaltic rock should have occurred originally or — granted the fact of their existence — it is not physically possible that they can have withstood the wear and tear of eons of time. How they have survived storms and the changing temperature, rain and the action of ice, is a mystery; yet there they are, as slender and as unworn by the passing of years as if time were a thing of no account.

There are four of these strange formations, if the steep eminence on which the cathedral is situated is also counted. This one is less characteristic and is more like a precipitous hill, the other three are the curiosities. On one is an ugly modern church, on another a gigantic statue of the Virgin and on the third an ancient chapel dedicated to St. Michael. This group of crowned, fingerlike rocks, about the bases of which clusters the red-roofed town, makes an unforgettable picture.

With J. T. comfortably settled in a potato patch, his stool between two rows and his feet between the next two below, the Younger Generation and I explored leisurely. With considerable difficulty we found the street leading to the foot of the rock of St. Michel, where a fierce mongrel held us at bay until a woman, working the endless coarse lace of this section, called him off. We found a stairway built so cleverly on and into the rock that it is practically invisible. Every jutting ledge and every indentation have been incorporated into it and the material of the outer sustaining wall is rock, hewn from the main portion, which harmonizes, consequently, both in color and in texture.

The oratory on the summit was built in the tenth, and its little ambulatory in the eleventh century. It was a true labor of love and a beautiful offering. Into this little building went, not only money and thought and devotion, but stiff backs, blistered hands and aching heads. Now we climb the two hundred and fifty steps with comparative ease, but in those days it meant first constructing the steps, then climbing them with every bit of material — stone, mortar, water even — to be used at the top.

The entrance is through a Romanesque door on which has been lavished a wealth of exquisite detail. The little chapel has no definite plan, for the top of this " Aiguille" is too small to hold a conventional design. There is a tiny rounded apse, and the body of the church is approximately square. The living rock has been leveled to partial smoothness and irregularly spaced columns with beautiful capitals support a simple roof. It is an ingenuous design perhaps, but sincere and absolutely straightforward. The height is considerable, making me wonder why a church dedicated to St. Michael is almost always on an elevation. Is it because — being an angel — they believed his winged self would feel more at home above the teeming world, while the saints — once mortal beings — could better endure its human, earthly quality?

To reach the Cathedral of Notre Dame one must climb a long and arduous hill which turns into a street of mounting steps, ending in the great wide flight of stone stairs which leads up and into the building. When the cathedral was originally built the entire summit of the volcanic hill was covered by the edifice, then later — the crowds of pilgrims having increased beyond its capacity — it became necessary to lengthen the nave. There was no ground to hold this new construction, yet somehow the problem had to be solved: so they built a substructure, a vast room under the new bays of the nave, making the floor far above the level of the street; then they carried the great flight of stairs up to the façade which finished the nave and formed the western wall of this lower building; then through the wall and up its entire height to a spot in front of the high altar. Two things were thus accomplished. The capacity of the cathedral was vastly increased, so that the miracle-working shrine could be seen by the greater number of pilgrims who were thus enabled to effect an entrance into the crowded interior; and also that those less fortunate, who had reached the stairs but for whom not an inch of space could be found within, might yet see — even though distantly — the altar and its sacred statue.

But whatever the size of the cathedral, it was still not large enough for the hordes who came at the height of the shrine's popularity. A frightful catastrophe marked the very earliest period of its existence.

The original Virgin of Le Puy was an ancient statue, said to have been carved by Jeremiah from cedar wood. The Arabs guarded it for years, during the course of which it became darker and darker until the word "black" was most appropriately used to describe its color. When Louis IX, better known as St. Louis, went to Egypt on his crusade, the statue was given him and he brought it back to France and presented it to his devoted city of Le Puy. Such a venerable statue, carved by such famous hands and preserved almost miraculously through the ages in an alien land, had an immediate and forceful appeal

LE PUY

THE CATHEDRAL OF NOTRE DAME AND THE CHAPEL OF ST. MICHEL

Size of the original etching, 9¾ inches by 13⅛ inches

to the imagination of a pious race. The news of it spread fast, accompanied by many stories of boons granted and of absolution bestowed. People hurried to see for themselves the wonder of which they had heard and to benefit by the tireless goodness already manifested to others. They overflowed the town, while the church could only hold a small fraction of their ever increasing numbers. They crowded the streets and steps until the solid mass of humanity was packed beyond free motion. It was a religious pilgrimage but even that did not keep it from being a mob, with the inevitable psychology of one. Someone stumbled and fell, and frightened feet trampled life from the luckless victim. Then was the moment in which to call upon the Virgin and to let her serenity hold their terrors in check, but human fears triumphed and a panic ensued which cost the lives of fourteen hundred persons.

This was on the occasion of the first " jubilé" at Le Puy, so called after an ancient Jewish custom of establishing a day of celebration on which all slaves were freed, all debts canceled and confiscated property was restored to the original owners. In mediaeval times the " jubilé" was a religious celebration of special papal indulgences, and this particular one of Le Puy took place when the anniversary of the Annunciation of the Virgin coincided with Good Friday. Anyone assisting in the services on this day at her shrine of special favor was assured of receiving unusual blessings and favors. Eager to avail themselves of the privilege, sometimes half frantic with fears which only the sympathetic Mary could quiet on just this one day, the pilgrims risked their temporal lives for a spiritual promise. There were similar accidents at every "jubilé"; two hundred anxious supplicants dead in one, thirty-three in another, ninety-five in still another; the records are tragic things. Finally in the seventeenth century the Pope decreed that the indulgence should last a week and the panic of these pilgrimages subsided with the greater leeway of time allowed.

The list of visitors from the earliest days of the shrine's popularity includes almost every great name of every age. Charlemagne came and Louis IX, donor of the miraculous image and — some say — of a thorn from the crown of Christ, was a frequent and honored pilgrim. Popes came, and cardinals, and kings from other lands. Charles VII had a vision vouchsafed him here which gave him courage to take up his campaign, and Isabelle Romée came with fervent prayers for the safety of her Warrior Maid. Her soul was troubled. A gentle dove, she had mothered an eaglet whose wide, strong wings clove the blue limitless spaces, bringing anxiety to her loving heart. Mary, with divine maternal understanding, gave her blessed resignation if not calm comfort.

Louis XI came on a less worthy mission. His conscience was burdened with cruelties and sins but his score with the Church was even. When danger threatened or the fear of death was upon him, he forgot the fact that he had obeyed every religious rule in letter if not in name, he forgot the pilgrimages he had made and he forgot the vows he had fulfilled, while he remembered only his injustices, his extortions and his murders. He came to Le Puy in dread for his mortal life and in deadly terror for his spiritual one; he conformed to the necessary forms and ceremonies and he confessed his sins with a curious mixture of fulsome detail and secrecy. The guileless city gave him a token of their appreciation of his gracious condescension, a little gold image of the sacred statue, which he wore in his hat; but I doubt if his royal head rested any more easily under it than under the crown of his inheritance.

Francis I also came, in a blaze of characteristic splendor. He brought his court with him, with all that meant of luxurious clothing and provender. What did he hope to get by this pilgrimage? Not sincere absolution, I am sure, for he was a frank and unashamed sinner, but perhaps a short-lived feeling of purity, a moment when the self-indulgent years slipped from him and he was a child once more, needing and asking for maternal counsel.

We mounted the steps which earlier pilgrims had passed on a different errand. They came to expiate a crime, to ask for a blessing, or to crave a favor. We modern pilgrims came looking for beauty, for the many flowered loveliness which their religious zeal had created. We found one expression of it here, not loveliness perhaps, but a certain grandeur tinged with a curious and exotic flavor.

The façade is very eastern in feeling; it speaks of southern suns and Mohammedan influences. The arches are round but the capitals of their supporting columns flare out, suggesting very much the Moorish form. The pediment has pointed gables in which are open arcades, and the materials of which it is built are the local stone and lava, arranged in bands of white and black and red. It is an alien type in France, but congruous somehow in this section where ancient volcanoes and more recent earthquakes have changed the face of the land from a suave countryside to a landscape full of unexpected features.

The stairs go through the façade as of old, but once in the building they change their course and branch, one side to the right into the transept of the church, the other to the left into the lovely cloisters. I did not find this interior sympathetic; it spoke a foreign tongue to me in which were blended the hot tones of the south and the cool cadences of the north, but then I am distinctly prejudiced against domical architecture.

The cloisters are really lovely, for the Byzantine style seems especially suited to an arcaded walk like this. The colors are gay but harmonious, the capitals beautifully designed and executed, and the grotesque which projects from the keystone of each arch is imaginative and vigorous. Each one contains legend, or religion, or humor.

To complete our modern pilgrimage we climbed the Rocher Corneille by the path which zigzags up the steep side. The statue of the Virgin which crowns the summit is interesting because it was cast from the cannon captured at Sebastopol, which Napoleon III presented to the citizens of Le Puy in recognition of their share in the successful campaign. It is not a beautiful statue, though its height adds one more emphasis to the curious silhouette and strange conglomeration which is Le Puy; from the star-encircled head one may get a glorious, if perilous view, down upon the cathedral, down upon the red-roofed town and down upon the Oratory of St. Michel.

We explored the city during the long twilights and found it intensely interesting rather than lovable, much as we had found its great cathedral. The inhabitants had been courteous as a whole but a little lacking in the spontaneous friendliness which we are accustomed to find in provincial France and which makes the give and take of daily contact a thing of gentle kindliness. These people were intent on definite aims, without time for all the little amenities of life; they were either selling something or were being paid for doing something. There were many mendicants and many who begged under a thin disguise of commerce. I had had a slightly apprehensive feeling during my entire stay, the subconscious feeling that comes with a lack of fundamental sympathy. There had been muttered grumblings when my purchases had not reached the anticipated size and the *gardien* of the cathedral museum had been definitely unpleasant. He had left the doors locked and had almost refused to let us go until he had exhibited lace made by " his sister or his cousin or his aunt" and which we were supposed to buy. Altogether, my mental attitude checked that state of joyous adventure in which I usually roam.

We wandered about one evening in the dark, narrow streets of the ancient section of the city and found enough pleasant sculptured bits, half seen by the light of a distant lamp, and nice doorways to quite allay my imagination. Suddenly we heard piercing and anguished screams from near at hand. My apprehensions seemed justified, a terrible thing must have occurred. Fearing everything, we hurried in the direction of the sound and found a comedy. A pig had escaped from a cart loaded with his brethren and the shrieks were merely his protesting squeals as he resisted capture, racing around and around an open square with boys and men in hot pursuit. The spell was broken and my black pall of fancied tragedy was gone and yet, as I look back, I find that Le Puy — with the notable exception of its exquisite Oratory — appealed strongly to my mind and stimulated my imagination but it left my heart untouched.

RODEZ

CROWNED by its great cathedral, Rodez rises from the vast plain which surrounds it like a magnificent ship at rest upon a green and placid ocean. It can be seen from afar, towering proudly, seeming to disdain the very existence of the lowlands and holding itself haughtily aloof from such base things as earth and stones. From a distance the strength and grandeur of mass and silhouette are impressive, while a nearer view reveals a church tower of exquisite loveliness which lends the added note of contrast.

We came to it one afternoon across a valley where the summer wheat rippled in the wind with changing, verdant lights. The road was level as we approached it until we reached the foot of the great craglike hill upon which the town is built, when it begins to rise in steep, broad curves, reaching the summit and the cathedral simultaneously. For here, as elsewhere, the church occupies the highest land just as it holds first place in the lives of its people.

Rodez claims great antiquity. It is said to have been settled about 2000 B.C. by a very ancient Celtic tribe called Ruthenians from the brilliant red color of their hair. This primitive race came here and gave its name to the town, a name which later became corrupted into the form now used. St. Martial, fighting Bishop of Limoges, brought Christianity to Rodez in the first century, but the new religion did not make much headway until the fifth, when St. Amans, a local bishop, completely converted the city. They seem always to have been a rather grim and taciturn race. Their remote situation withdrew them from easy contact with the world and made their retreat a fortress town coveted by all. They withstood sieges or were conquered, and they were finally divided into separate units, the Cité belonging to the bishop and the Bourg to the domain of the Count of Rodez. This brought about a curious situation. The two parts of the town were definitely separated in every way, with high double walls between them, for apparently neither side relied sufficiently on the good faith of the other to put trust in a single barrier. These walls were pierced by fortified gates closed at nightfall, through which no one might pass without the proper credentials. It was brother against brother and family against family.

The first church of Notre Dame, built inside this military defense, fell in

1276. Raymond de Calmont, a farseeing bishop, had anticipated the catastrophe, though what cracked masonry or what forboding noises gave him warning we have not learned. We do know, however, that, fearing trouble, he hastily removed to a place of safety the sacred relics and the altar of Deusdedit, the bishop who built the first sanctuary at the beginning of the Christian era. The Romanesque church crashed to the ground and only a fragment of it was left standing, but the bishop, quite undaunted, preached to a responsive flock the message that the accident was a blessing rather than a tragedy. They could now construct, in the Gothic style which was flooding France with a tide of new beauty, a cathedral worthy of the Virgin's notice. The people responded with money and labor, and work went on rapidly for a while, then dropped off, and another two centuries went by before the project was completed. This naturally brought about changes in style. The west façade was built actually on the ramparts and is fortresslike in design and feeling up as far as the lovely Gothic window, which in turn is surmounted by a Renaissance motive of a much later date, while the simple base of the original tower ends in a superstructure which is delicately, richly Flamboyant in quality.

It is endlessly interesting to me to trace a little the effect of physical limitations, and the character of a people, upon an architectural monument. The west façade of Rodez was constructed upon a military barrier because the line of that fortified wall came at the spot to which the builders wished to extend the church. The massive foundations destined for defense must have influenced their design, just as the height of it precluded any entrance at that end. Coupled with that was the nature of the inhabitants; they were industrious but poor, dwellers in a hard land which yielded a mere livelihood yet no abundance. They were raising their cathedral gladly, from their own deep feeling of religious fervor and to the glory of the Madonna, but the cost of it was a heavy burden on them. So they built it structurally strong and fine but they eliminated ornamentation and finishings for a time of greater financial ease. In consequence we find the original portions severe and simple, only the later additions or changes are more elaborate and gracious. The façade sums up this transition. In the main it is almost forbidding in the austerity of its straight lines and the plain surfaces of its inception, while the culminating gable is a product of the florid Renaissance period.

Some enthusiasts acclaim the tower to the northeast as the most beautiful in France. With that of Chartres and St. Ouen's "Crown of Normandy" in our memories, we could not fully agree, though it surely has the right to reign

RODEZ

TOWER OF NOTRE DAME

Size of the original etching, 12 inches by 5 inches

John Taylor Arms - 1927

supremely in the south. Even beside the greatest examples it is very lovely. The square foundation was the base of the original tower, which terminated in a wooden spire. In 1510 some workmen were making repairs on it when, by an act of gross carelessness, they started a fire which caught and spread with terrifying rapidity. Thoroughly alarmed, they endeavored to extinguish it but with no success; the neighboring townspeople hurried to assist but the flames outstripped their efforts and the recently completed cathedral was in danger of destruction. Human means had failed and their church seemed doomed until the bishop bethought him of the relics of St. Amans. They were brought to the scene with a haste which precluded all ceremony, and as they reached the spot the flames died out suddenly and completely. The church was saved and only the cold ashes of a ruined spire remained to tell the tale. Even this fact had a silver lining. The wooden steeple had never seemed as dignified as the rest of the building and the resourceful bishop François d'Estaing raised the money for a more elaborate structure of a permanent material. The new tower was fittingly named for him and a stone in its walls commemorates the destruction of the first and the erection of its successor.

This lovely tower is a memorial of which a bishop or, for that matter, any saint might well be proud. It is the personification of grace, a quality which needs strength as well as delicacy to reach its highest development. Both attributes are found here to a marked degree. The solid base is massive, yet it merges almost imperceptibly into the extreme delicacy at the top. The transition from the square of the lower part to the octagon of the upper is cleverly handled by the use of small turrets of fragile decoration, and the graduation of scale and type of ornament is almost faultless.

Because of the lack of a western portal one enters by the shallow transepts. The interior is plain, almost severe, but dignified and impressive in its simplicity. It is the logical church of a reserved, uncompromising people who built for strength and durability and who worshiped in the beauty of holiness rather than in a bewildering wealth of architectural detail. The columns are clustered piers which terminate in ring capitals, the vaulting is essentially a structural feature and the whole feeling is one of simple taste, simply expressed. Yet through it all one feels the fighting strength of a religious faith which was a vital part of the life of the community and which showed itself in this central, well-loved cathedral.

The tower we had come so far to see and to draw was unfortunately covered by scaffolding on three of its sides. The fourth side was free and there we could see and study the wealth of detail which we knew only from descriptions and pictures. We were thankful for this unimpeded view which yet made us regret the more the covered portions and which increased the difficulty of a drawing. We explored the radiating streets with no success; where everything else harmonized only a blind side of the belfry showed. One quiet backwater of an alley offered a view of its unhidden beauty, but with so much of the lower part masked by foreground buildings that it barely peeped above them. There was no window from the greater height of which this defect would disappear, and J. T. nearly despaired. Then, taking the proprietor aside, he borrowed the hotel stepladder. In the morning he left, bearing it upon his shoulder to the intense interest of the inhabitants, and in the evening he marched back again with the same burden. During the day he sat upon the extreme top, serenely above the groups of curious children and adults, away from their staring looks and whispered comments and with only a slight feeling of uneasiness that, in their anxiety to see what this quite mad man was about, they might upset ladder, artist, drawing-board and all.

It was the fourteenth of July and that night there was a festival, with a concert in the park and fireworks. The streets were decorated, and when it was dark, flares of red fire were lit in the squares. The strange light touched the blank façade of the cathedral magically, accentuating the sculptures and making black shadows even darker. It flamed brightly, suggesting the old wars and sieges, the conflagration in the tower and even the hair of the ancient inhabitants; then went out, leaving the church to dream on, serene and undisturbed.

ALBI

THE cathedral of Albi is dedicated to Ste. Cécile, the most utterly unsuitable and inappropriate saint in the whole calendar. She was a gentle person who loved music and flowers and all the spiritual things of life, yet they built here in her honor a church which is virtually a fortress. It is of red brick and the walls are high, with narrow, grudging windows and semicircular buttresses. From the southern side springs a baldachin of white stone, which, added in the sixteenth century, is as inharmonious with the rest of the structure as the life of the peaceful saint is with the spirit and ambitions of the warlike prelates who constructed the church.

We arrived in Albi on a July day of intense heat. Prudence suggested waiting for a cooler hour but eager impatience counseled an immediate exploration. Sensible people had forsaken the streets, leaving them to the fierce glare and brief, hard shadows of noonday; only a poor dog was in sight, shaking and shivering with illness.

An empty street brought us to the cathedral, its brick walls hot in the sun, and against them the whiteness of the carved porch was in startling contrast. In the uncompromising light the elaborate carving which covers it stood out in high relief, revealing every beauty of line and detail. It seemed a frail drawbridge to an ecclesiastical fortress, with its fifty steps flung lightly up against the wall of the cathedral and terminating in the baldachin, whose strength was belied by its delicate ornament. Such a narrow way could be easily guarded or, if need arose, it might be sufficiently demolished to leave the church inaccessible. This southern entrance is a most unusual and beautiful example of the Flamboyant style. It consists of a fortified gate, a flight of steps, a porch called locally a baldachin because of its resemblance to the canopied motive used in many church interiors, and an elaborate portal. Sculptured detail has been carried to a superlative degree, yet the scale is so perfect and the design so well executed that there is no sense of crowding. It is a bit of rare beauty in which scenes from church history, local saints and the armorial bearings of the Bishops of Albi have been used as interesting central features, and about which every detail and every motive of the most elaborate style of architecture known to man have been worked into a frame of rhythmic loveliness.

We passed into the church by way of this portal, through walls immensely thick. Built to resist the onslaught of man, they also serve as an impenetrable barrier against heat. We stepped into an interior cold as a vault and again we felt a shock of contrast and incongruity. We found the inner surface of those forbidding walls excavated to form lateral chapels, gay with Italian frescoes, while across the nave was a rood screen unquestionably the largest and perhaps the most elaborate in all of France.

Here there is an endless wealth of material for study. This jubé, the choir screen and the stalls, leave an impression of intricate design and delicate execution out of the mass of which no one feature predominates. The plan of the church is curious. There is only a single aisle, due probably to the extreme thickness of the walls which have encroached so upon the width, and the sanctuary is at the western instead of the eastern end. The west façade has no portal but is grim and blank and forbidding, while within is an inadequate high altar. The eastern end is closed off behind the high stone tracery of the screen. A sacristan unlocks a door leading to it that one may see the glory of its sculptures, but it no longer serves as a part of the living church.

The frescoes are especially interesting. They cover the walls of the chapels and the vaulting and are remarkably well preserved. There is great variation in them, with historic or legendary representations separated by elaborate Renaissance decorative motives or curious grotesques.

Beautiful though it is — all this elaboration of sculpture and fresco — it seemed a superficial ornamentation rather than a spontaneous expression of religious fervor which must show itself in terms of beauty. The mural artists came from Italy — imported to execute a commission — the stone-cutting is overwrought, and there is something almost insincere about it all. I felt the iron hand in the velvet glove and, personally, would have preferred this fortress church in the uncompromising simplicity of its unadorned martial need, instead of veiled in a softness which does not and cannot express its character. It is an incongruity which even the great beauty of the design and execution cannot keep from making a false note.

We wandered about so long that we quite forgot the weather in this cool, dim interior. Conscious that height was a dominant feature of the Cathedral of Albi, we determined to climb the tower for a comprehensive, commanding view. We went up an endless stairway in the great walls, finally emerging on the parapet which encircles the roof. It seemed wise to follow it around, thus gaining a better idea of the dimensions of the building. We started, and the

ALBI

THE CATHEDRAL OF STE. CÉCILE

Size of the original etching, 9¾ inches by 10¼ inches

ALBI-1926-

John Taylor Arms 1927

heat descended upon us like a living, menacing thing. On one side there was a considerable drop to the roof of the church, on the other, through the crenellated parapet, we had interrupted views of the spreading town and country far below us. The air was full of vibrating waves which rose and rose and threatened to envelop us. We looked dizzily about and realized that the plan of the church was so appallingly simple that we were lost. There were some turrets and the great west tower, but where we had come up, or where we should later descend, was beyond our immediate comprehension. We turned our footsteps towards the last eminence and once more embarked upon a lengthy climb.

This tower is really extraordinary. It must have been purely a defensive structure originally, with its blank, strong walls and massive construction. The upper part is Gothic, another surprising feature in this edifice of contrasts. The style has been cleverly adapted to the unusual material in which it is executed, and forms a lighter but harmonious termination to a heavy, purposeful foundation.

From the summit we looked down upon the river Tarn four hundred feet below us. The city of Albi is built upon a ridge, on the highest and farthest point of which stands the cathedral. The tower is seventy-eight meters high, an altitude which, added to the abrupt line of the cliff, makes an almost sheer drop to the river below and offers an extensive view. From one side we looked down upon the city where the smoke from many factory chimneys hung heavily in the breathless air, from the other down to the roofs of the old Archiepiscopal Palace and into the protected garden where the bishops used to walk. They felt safe there, with their fortified home and cathedral behind them and the unscalable precipice in front.

They needed security, for they lived in warring times. The Albigensian heresy took its name from Albi, where it started and which was the storm center of its brief and suffering life. Few of these so-called heretics lived to perpetuate their beliefs or their aims. In the eyes of the victorious Church they were worse than infidels, an abomination to the elect and a manifestation of Satan. The records are biased and an impersonal judgment is difficult, but it seems fair to suppose that this was not an anti-Christian uprising but a revulsion against the practices and corruptions of the mediaeval Church. The dissenters must have had cogent reasons, for thoughtful people joined the original group and it took a papal bull, a special inquisition and a long and bitter campaign to suppress them. I want to forget the details of horror and injustice, the bare outlines are a sufficient blot on the progress of Christianity. The Bishops of Albi were zealous in their pursuit of the heretics, and Simon de Montfort, whose dark shadow lies blackly across the sunny heights of Carcassonne, finally crushed the revolt. He accomplished this result by killing every possible participant, one of the most brutal and most ruthless persecutions of history.

The hour was getting late and the hard light was softening. We came down the tower and found the stairs leading to the nave. The highly decorated interior no longer looked in diverting contrast, it was a mask to hide dreadful things, a veil only the more sinister because of its light and graceful aspect. We emerged on to the porch and came down to the street where the black shadow of the church stretched forth, symbolical of the dark power of those mediaeval days. I shivered and hurried into the comforting sunshine. What an anachronism that faith founded preëminently on love should have been so misinterpreted by religious zeal that the exponents of one sect hated and tortured and killed the exponents of another!

In those days of ceaseless strife the Bishops of Albi made themselves as safe as possible from attack. They built their palace as a fort only slightly less impregnable than the adjoining church, into which they might retire as a last stronghold in time of direst need. They successfully withstood many sieges, but what safeguard did they have against the blood of their innocent victims which cried out against them? Or what defenses have their memories now against the indictment of the world?

BOURG–EN–BRESSE

THE name of Bourg-en-Bresse suggests to the average French mind white chickens, the famous breed whose fine, firm meat forms the basis of their epicurean dinners.

We were awakened our first morning there by a squawking and clucking and crowing, and hurrying to the window we gazed down upon an open square which looked as if a premature winter had covered the ground with snow. The chickens were there in all the purity of their glistening white plumage and in such quantities that we doubted if all of France could consume them. As a matter of fact, only Paris is favored with these much coveted fowl and thousands and thousands are sent daily to satisfy the delicate palates of that hungry city.

We stepped over hens, and around hens, and almost on hens as we threaded a difficult way through this crowded, protesting market; then suddenly the noise and bustle were behind us and we found ourselves on a dusty, dreary boulevard whose long emptiness led nowhere, so far as we could see. We walked and walked and presently we came to our objective, the Église de Brou. I doubt if any church has a worse or more unsuitable setting. The surroundings are neither country nor town, but a dull combination of the two, and about the grounds on which it stands is a blank brick wall, whose empty, featureless expanse successfully hides the lower portion of the church entirely and so cuts the height that the effect of the whole is lost.

The façade is, I think, the strangest within my knowledge. The portal is low and disproportionately wide, large windows fill the wall above it, the pediment is pierced by four motives of openwork tracery — one round and three triangular ones — and tiny turrets complete the gable. There are lovely balustrades of exquisite workmanship and many of the individual features are very fine, but the façade is not pleasing as a whole; it is an example of the decadence of a style. The necessary restraint is lacking, one feels that the flower of true beauty has bloomed too far and that its wide parted petals are already dropping to decay.

We were disappointed, for, in spite of some beautiful details, there was no visible composition here. We walked around to the side; the grass of the enclosure was dry and powdery under our feet, insects hummed drowsily and camomile daisies gave forth a pungent odor when crushed by the steps of our passing. We came to the northern door and found a transept so exquisite in design that our quest was ended then and there.

The church was built by Marguerite of Austria to contain three tombs, and the story of its construction is found in a complicated mass of letters, orders of sums paid for material and records of wages. Through the dry facts run threads of human interest where ambition and jealousy, extravagance and meanness, and a woman's nature weave a living pattern.

Marguerite of Bourbon made a vow that if her husband, Duke Philip of Savoy, recovered from a hunting accident, she would build a chapel. Her prayer was granted but her promise was long in fulfillment, although work was started and partially carried on in the cathedral in the town. Her son, Philibert the Fair, married Marguerite of Austria, but their life and happiness together were brief. The loss of their only child when newly born was a grief from which she never recovered, and when her husband died soon afterwards she, in turn, vowed to erect a building to house his tomb and hers. With an efficiency not otherwise exhibited, she decided to fulfill her mother-in-law's incompleted promise and build the three memorials together. Pressure was brought to bear upon her that she should carry on the work already begun, but the young widow declared, with that gentle stubbornness so hard to combat and with tears in her pretty eyes, that she regretted excessively her inability to fall in with these desires but that this would not conform with her vow.

So the church of Brou was undertaken and in 1532, after twenty-six years of construction, it was completed. Soon after her husband's death, Marguerite of Austria was summoned to act as regent over Flanders, so that all of her directing was done by correspondence and she died just before the building was finished. She never saw the church on which she had lavished so much thought and so much money but her body rests where she wanted it to, beside her husband and in the midst of beauty.

The names of three men stand out as of those responsible for this building, although in the mass of statements and contradictions it is difficult to get at the correct facts; Jean Perréal the architect, Van Boghen of Flanders and perhaps Michel Colombe, that great artist who designed his own finest memorial when he produced the tomb of Francis II, Duke of Brittany, at Nantes. This change of designer probably accounts for a lack of harmony in the building,

BOURG

ÉGLISE DE BROU, BOURG–EN–BRESSE

Size of the original etching, 8⅞ inches by 4⅛ inches

Eglise de Brou

John Taylor Arms 1927

but who can cavil when the result, in the interior and in the sculpture, is one in which sheer virtuosity of achievement has rarely, if ever, been excelled?

The three memorial monuments, for the appropriate housing of which this church of Brou was built, are in the choir. That of one Marguerite is to the right, that of the other Marguerite to the left, while Philibert's is in the center. The mausoleum of Marguerite of Bourbon is a sculptured niche in which rests her marble effigy. The design of the whole may be a little heavy and over-elaborate, but the frieze of small hooded figures across the base of the tomb is incomparably lovely. The attitude of each one is thoughtful and full of grace, the drapery falls in sweeping lines and every tiny face, hidden in the depths of its deep drawn veil, is as carefully portrayed as if it were the principal motive. We had to kneel and look up, light in hand, in order even to see them, yet not one is carelessly done. Each is a perfect face, depicting emotion and with a distinct feeling of portraiture in it.

Marguerite of Austria lies under a double tomb in which the upper figure represents her in the full panoply of her state robes, a crown upon her head and a sleeping dog beneath her regal feet. The lower figure shows her as she was when death overtook her, tranquilly asleep, her long hair rippling over her shoulders and the sculptured material which covers her hanging in simple, half careless folds.

Philibert rests in the center, son of one, husband of the other Marguerite, whose promises to high heaven culminated in his tomb, just as their hopes and ambitions were buried in it also. On it has been lavished a wealth of detail and a perfection of execution. Similar to his wife's, his memorial has two statues of him. The higher one is guarded by solicitous cherubs who bend lovingly over his recumbent figure, with the symbols of his temporal power grouped about them. The lower one lies on his deathbed, bereft of worldly trappings and half hidden by the elaborate features of the openwork base. The former portion is Renaissance in feeling, the latter Gothic of the most ornate period. Separated by arched motives of involved and delicate tracery, are small figures of Sibyls in varied attitudes. They are exquisite and significant sculptures of poignant expression.

All of the interior of the church is just as elaborate, with an intricate rood screen incorporating the initials " P " and " M," an ante-chamber with a sculptured fireplace, carved choir stalls and a profusion of other detail. We felt that, fine as each individual thing might be, it would have been more impressive had

[123]

this part been simpler, making a severer setting for the jewel-like beauties of the tombs.

While we were in the church one of the rare thunderstorms of France came up. We were divided between the desire to be out of a high building under those conditions and the wish to stay and see more fully some of the details of the interior. We stayed, and with flashlight and taper examined the sculptures which the hurrying clouds were endeavoring to hide. Thunder roared, rain and hail beat tempestuously against the windows and lightning flashed through some blue glass of unusual color with a brilliant light well worth remembering. The storm passed as quickly as it had come and we emerged into a wet world of glistening raindrops. Standing upon the quaint sundial set into the ground before the church, the dazzling sunshine cast our shadows clear and black against the hour of four. We looked back at the building. A lifetime of loving thought had been expended upon its construction and the world is the richer by a monument, not alone of an individual, but also one of beauty.

MENDE

WE have always felt that we discovered Mende, and no amount of proof to the contrary will ever serve to disabuse us of this fixed idea. Having left Le Puy one fine morning, with the firm intention of reaching Rodez that night, the car developed dirty spark-plugs and various trifling ailments which so delayed us that when we limped into a town which offered a possible looking hotel, and a more than possible looking garage, we decided that the appointed moment had come for a pause in our progress.

Beyond mechanical repairs we expected nothing of the town, which seemed modern and uninteresting, but J. T., who is chronically optimistic, had seen a church steeple and so, with dinner barely over, he started in search of that always-possible subject, no matter how unlikely the place may seem. He found it — a Gothic bridge, dedicated to Notre Dame, across a barely moving, dreamy river, and beyond an unspoiled, quite unbelievably lovely town. The interesting spire of the cathedral could be seen above the gabled houses, and far off a steep mountain side, vineyard clad.

So there we stayed for the space of time needed to make a drawing, and, as the needle to the pole, the Younger Generation and I gravitated first of all to the cathedral. A nice *gardien* met us almost at the door with the suggestion that we climb the tower, which we decided was an excellent idea. As we walked across the church he said to me, as one who states a fact, " You are English," and when I denied it and mentioned our nationality, he nodded his head sagely and said, " Oh yes, but the languages are quite similar, I believe." I hastened to inform him that, except for slight variations in pronunciation, the two were identical, but my words lacked all effect; he merely smiled and replied indulgently that he was sure the resemblance between the two tongues was very noticeable.

About this time he made the discovery that the Younger Generation both understood and spoke French, as well as the fact that it was tremendously keen to see everything there was to be seen, and to understand what things were, and why. So with the very beautiful sympathy which the best type of Frenchman has in such abundance for a child and its enthusiasms, he proceeded to take us through every nook and corner of the church, with a greater thoroughness than anything which had heretofore befallen us. He opened doors in little rooms part way up the tower. In one the ancient archives had been kept until moved to safer and dryer surroundings. Another, lined by shelves, seemed to be a sort of study, and in a third were the works of the great clock whose dial was far above us. It whirred and ticked prodigiously and we felt somehow close to the heart of the building, a strong and understanding heart of tireless energy.

He took us on to odd little unexpected balconies, he pointed out the structural strength which certain apparently purely ornamental features gave, and all the while we climbed steadily but leisurely the spiral staircase, worn to a dangerous unevenness by centuries of mounting and descending footsteps. At length we found ourselves at the top, with a magnificent view on every side. We could see, towards the north from which we had come the day before, the strange mountains whose rich ore deposits creep out in dingy scars upon their sides, and, to the south, the conjunction of the Lot and the Tarn and the steeper hills which close in those picturesque rivers. It is from Mende that many people start on the trip through the Gorges of the Tarn, that natural wonder-spot whose wild beauty and grim grandeur have made it famous far outside of France. At our feet the town nestled closely about the church, one side of it skirting the river, much as a child who paddles in cold water with daring toes yet shrinks against the comforting maternal knee. The Lot, seen from here, was a gleaming ribbon meandering lazily through cultivated fields, with earth-colored villages dotting its banks at scattered intervals.

After the view came the bells, massive bronze things hung in a wooden framework which seemed alarmingly frail. Our guide, philosopher and friend (who had by now proved himself endowed with all these qualities) explained that it was necessary to climb all these two hundred and fifty-three steps to ring them, and that they were rung for every service. "Other churches," he said, "have various devices; some are rung by hand from below, some by electricity, but these of St. Pierre are still sounded in the old-fashioned way. I am getting old," he continued, "and the stairs are growing hard for me. Yesterday, being Sunday, there were extra masses and more visitors, and I had to go up eight different times." "Are there many visitors?" I asked. "Yes, indeed," came his prompt reply, "many, often as many as three or four in a day! You know, Madame, our cathedral is quite unique. It is less well-known than some of the great churches of the large cities, but for its façade and this

CATHEDRAL OF NOTRE DAME, SEEN FROM THE PONT NOTRE DAME

MENDE

CATHEDRAL OF NOTRE DAME, SEEN FROM THE PONT NOTRE DAME

Size of the original etching, 8⅛ inches by 12⅝ inches

John Taylor Arms 1921

beautiful tower, it ranks as one of the finest in the opinion of those who know."
Again the naïve, lovely egotism of possession.

In the course of time we came down from our sojourn in the skies, but leisurely still. This time our guide unlocked and opened yet another door and took us out under the timbered roof, and over the vaulting of the nave. That was one of the most interesting and enlightening things I had ever seen. I had never heretofore quite realized the great space between the high, steep-pitched roof of a Gothic edifice, which one sees from the outside, and the so much flatter ceiling which one sees from the interior. It was quite unfinished-looking, merely the uneven stone vaulting, roughly plastered. It is from here that the light before the high altar is hung. A slender wire which passes through a small hole in the ceiling holds the lamp so very far below.

Having seen this part of the church and the rooms leading out of the tower, it was easy to understand the quantity of space, unseen and usually unsuspected, in a church the size of Notre Dame de Paris. No wonder Esmeralda could be hidden there so successfully, that plots and counterplots had room in which to hatch and grow, and I half expected to see the ghost of a local Quasimodo peep at me between hunched shoulders from some dusty corner.

This cathedral of St. Pierre is not a great architectural monument, it may not even be a very good one. I, personally, cannot criticize it dispassionately, any more than I could the features of a kindly, lovable face. Perhaps our intimate, unhurried visit biased our opinion, but whatever the cause, I look back on a gracious church of wide spaces, on a façade of more than a little interest, and on a slender tower, delicately true.

J. T. was too far away to take the time to walk home for luncheon and the car was in the garage, so when the noon hour struck and thoughts of food came unbidden to our minds, we lunched; then the Younger Generation and I set forth to carry sustenance to our workingman like any other dutiful family. A cool bottle of water, well wrapped against the heat, two dainty rolls in the making of which the French excel, and a traveling-cup, constituted our burden. The glare from white houses, and the wide, dusty avenues of the newer section, soon gave place to the restful shadows cast by high, vine-covered walls edging the narrow streets of the older part, and we gratefully kept in this shade as we zigzagged down in what we hopefully believed to be the right direction. That is one comforting thing about a river; if one keeps on descending, sooner or later one is almost bound to come upon it, unless by some unfortunate error in reckoning one has started down the wrong side of the town. All went well this time, and we crossed the three-arched bridge which rises to such a steep point in the center, and soon were installed on the other side of the river, looking back at the town whose maze of streets we had just successfully threaded and at the lovely tower which we had so lately ascended.

Below the bridge the river widened into a shallow pool; the water was clear and the sun's rays struck through it to the sandy bottom, making every inch of it perfectly and completely visible, yet two men with a good-sized net seined that spot industriously for several hours. Needless to say, they did not get a thing, not even a sucker or a blade of grass. I wonder, did they really expect to? Presently the shadows lengthened, a little cool breeze sprang up and gently rippled the surface of the water. The drawing was finished and the inevitable knapsack packed and strapped up, and in the evening light we retraced our steps, leaving behind us the scene itself but carrying with us the memory of it as a bit of tranquil beauty, difficult to surpass.

BOURGES

BOURGES is the exact center of France, a fact which gives its residents considerable satisfaction. It goes back to Roman days, to Julius Caesar, wise administrator and ruthless general, to whose training and judgment and foresight the country owes its first great walls and fortifications, the nucleus of the roads which now cover the land like a web and the foundations of its laws and customs. But his cruelty is traditional in Bourges to this day.

It is an ancient city still, and an important one. The principal streets are full of modern life and commerce, yet a few steps on either side one comes to old houses of half-timber work, to mansions of mediaeval splendor and to the Cathedral of St. Étienne, one of the most magnificent of all ecclesiastical edifices. With the beauty of Rheims now only a matter of record and glorified memory, the cathedral of Bourges has advanced one place in the ranks of the very great. It deserves to stand with Chartres, Amiens and Notre Dame de Paris, and it is therefore a matter for some surprise to find it so well known by reputation yet comparatively little by personal experience. The true Frenchman appreciates it and is familiar with its wealth of stained glass and its architectural loveliness, but the foreigner often passes it by on his hurried way to other places whose trifle more of fame makes of them tourist centers. Perhaps this fact gives to the city of Bourges some of its charm, while it certainly adds to one's peaceful enjoyment of its cathedral.

The origin of this building goes back into dim antiquity, as does the town. It is said to date from the first days of Christianity, when St. Ursin brought from Rome the sacred relics of Stephen, first martyr in the cause of the new faith. Ursin was a missionary and to his efforts was due the conversion of the region of Berry. At this time Leocade, governor of Acquitania, was becoming more and more interested in the novel doctrines which the other preached, and offered him his own palace at Bourges for a sanctuary. Here were placed the earthly remains of St. Stephen and here they stayed, as far as we know, until in 380 there was built a new church of greater size and elaboration in which to house them. The present Gothic cathedral was constructed in the twelfth and thirteenth centuries, though its enrichment is due to many succeeding years.

Each generation has added of its wealth in glass or in treasures, in chapels or in carvings, until we find it today a history in stone of man's faith and his expression of it. Three features alone would suffice to make it a noteworthy building: the beautiful porch with its five deep portals, the great length of the nave, unbroken by any line of outjutting transepts, and the magnificent apse, worthy to be compared with any.

We originally came to Bourges while France was still to us an almost undiscovered land. When we had recovered from the first feeling of bewilderment engendered by the overwhelming mass of beauty by which we found ourselves surrounded, these three features predominated in our minds. We have been back again and yet again, but the feeling persists that, no matter what less obvious loveliness may have revealed itself, these are the outstanding achievements of the unknown builders of this great cathedral.

The general plan of the church is so simple as to be almost elementary; it is a vast rectangle whose eastern end is rounded to contain the sanctuary, but there are subtleties, such as the shape and placing of the radiating apsidal chapels, which place it with the great designs of all times.

The most radical departure from convention is the elimination of both transepts, which greatly increases the effect of length, a dimension very considerable in actuality. As we looked along the southern wall the church seemed to go on indefinitely, with its strong buttresses repeating each other in simple silhouette and in rhythmic procession. We were reminded of a sea whose waves, rising and falling in uninterrupted sequence, progress steadily onward. As I look at my composite mental picture of it, made up of many visual ones, I always see in it that combined quality of strength and motion, that feeling of life which is never completely still but which goes on and on interminably.

In lieu of transepts there are lateral doors which were part of the original church, preceded by porches of a lacelike beauty. There are sculptured scenes and statues and Gothic tracery in profusion, and the cusps between the outer pillars are deeper and more ornate than any I remember. It was here that a little lady accepted an assisting arm down the rather steep steps, and, as I walked along a little farther beside her, inquired about America and my wanderings. It seems she had been once to Paris during the life of her late husband, but she had found it crowded and uncongenial and had never cared to repeat the experience. She asked about other French cathedrals which I had seen and ended with the gentle remark, half question, half statement, that she was sure I had never seen a lovelier than this of St. Étienne at Bourges. For though she

John Taylor Arms 1925

could hardly call herself traveled, yet she had talked with many learned people who considered this the finest of Gothic edifices. I looked up at the west façade and felt inclined to agree with her wise friends.

The five portals correspond with the five aisles of the interior and they are modeled to the point of jeweled brilliance. The profundity of their penetration casts deep shadows of luminous darkness, in which chiseled surfaces make a play of light. There is a graceful arcade, a tier of Gothic canopies beneath which only some of the sainted figures remain, bands of sculptured scenes in the tympanums, rows of angels and saints in the reveals of the great arches and pierced stone designs in the gables above. It is a pattern of light and shade and a revelation in delicacy and in feeling.

If it is beautiful now, what must it have been at the height of its perfection! We usually blame the Revolution for all iconoclastic acts and the biased recorder, himself a descendant of those guilty of the depredations, is loath to condemn too bitterly the action, while he sympathizes perhaps with the actuating motive. For personal freedom is still the Frenchman's slogan. That being the case, I was interested to read the vindictive writings of outraged humanity on the subject of similar and equally disastrous destruction by a group of Protestants in 1562. Under Gabriel de Lorges, Count of Montgomery, they secretly entered the city and sought to destroy the cathedral. The records gleefully point out that in the course of their wicked work they put a rope about the neck of a large statue in order to pull it down, but divine wrath caused things to go wrong, the statue slipped and crushed to death several of the impious men. They destroyed much and they looted the church of its treasure, then the Revolution added its quota of wrecking and the only wonder is that the cathedral survives with so much of its original beauty.

The interior is remarkable for its great length and its famous windows. The latter are like a wonderful circle of flaming banners hung about the walls, their colors blending or contrasting with a brilliant radiance. Books have been written on them alone, in which each pane of glass, each storied subject, is a matter for careful study. They well repay the time thus spent on them, but for us who pass more quickly, to whom the windows, the church, the city are each one piece in the vast pattern of the beauty of France, they live as a band of varied light.

The cathedral, like the town, is inextricably associated with the life of its greatest citizen, Jacques Cœur. He built the sacristy with its lovely door, and on the site of the old sacristy a chapel with a curious niche in the wall where he and his wife might kneel to pray. She is buried there and there he hoped to lie, but an unkind fate willed it otherwise.

The son of a furrier, he early showed signs of great promise and in time became a merchant and sailed to distant lands, even making a pilgrimage to the Holy Land. He was connected with the local mint, an institution which at that period acted as the old-time miller, taking a percentage of the material carried to it for conversion. People brought gold or silver or baser metals and the mint stamped them, keeping a certain proportion for the king and a lesser amount for itself. There were naturally many abuses of the custom; money was debased by the addition of too much alloy or the face value of the coin was changed to the advantage of the sovereign.

Charles VII, dispossessed of a great part of his realm, generally lived in Bourges. He offered the position of "Argentier" to Jacques Cœur, who assumed it in spite of the great dangers attendant on the post. They also say he stipulated one condition. He had come to see Charles and was horrified at the shabby, even poverty-stricken appearance of the king and his court; so when he accepted, it was on the understanding that the first sum of money should go towards proper raiment for his sovereign and his queen. This may be true or not, but the existence of their poverty is an historical fact.

This great financial genius took over a country tottering on the verge of bankruptcy; he established a system of banks, stabilized the coinage, encouraged commerce and provided the money by the means of which, and by the aid of Jeanne d'Arc, Charles VII regained so much of his kingdom. But his fate almost resembled that of the other martyr to this fickle, faithless king. After years of prosperity Jacques Cœur was accused of having poisoned Agnes Sorel, the royal mistress; his fortune was seized and he was subjected to torture and to imprisonment. Their end gained and his money in the hands of his enemies and his one-time grateful monarch, he finally escaped, perhaps from Poitiers, and is said to have stayed a while at Limoges with a son, a canon of the cathedral there. He died poor and virtually in exile on a crusade to the land where he had once sailed as a wealthy, honored merchant.

He was the great Frenchman of that era and the charges against him were absurd fabrications of bitter and revengeful people. They killed their future prosperity for immediate gain, though even then they did not realize the enormity of their mistake. He was a fine character and a pious churchman and his gifts to the cathedral brought him great joy. He so much loved the Church that he dedicated two sons to her service. His eldest, Jean, was made nominal bishop of Bourges at twenty-three, although the legal age for the office was thirty years. A special dispensation, due to his father's influence, overrode the ruling and he was consecrated at the age of twenty-seven at St. Étienne with great ceremony. It was during his bishopric that his father built the sacristy and chapel.

Under the choir lies the crypt, one of the largest and most beautiful of all. To reach it one descends an inclined path where brackets of curious grotesques support the vaulting. The central part of this substructure seems very ancient; it probably belonged to the older building while the outer portion is that which was constructed when the church was enlarged. It is a place of dim and reverent feeling, the architecture is sturdy and simple and the vaulting low and massive. There is a tomb here, that of Duke John, the recumbent figure scratched and marred with names written in pencil or deeply incised with the point of a knife. The dignity of it as a whole remains but the surface, smoothed by time, is irreparably destroyed. The sixteenth and eighteenth century vandals could hardly have exceeded the destruction. The modern vandal penetrates as boldly into the deepest, the most seemingly sacred recesses.

Our walks took us into sections of delightful quaintness. There was one quarter, down among sluggish canals, where the streets went off at curious angles and old houses were the rule rather than the exception. Here was the old church of Notre Dame, defaced and worn but still in the center of the people and in their hearts. Another part of the city had a square as ancient, perhaps, but better cared for. The houses were in good order and boasted a certain amount of fresh paint and stain. One lifted twin gables above the line of its eaves, high and pointed, another was shingled in bands and another stood at an angle on its corner with a sort of knowing slant.

We saw the Hotel Lallemant, one-time residence of wealth and splendor, beautiful still but almost unused. A trout hatchery is in the garden; through the various trays clear water runs day and night, a placid and undisturbed symbol of the present peaceful life. The home of Jacques Cœur always had a strong appeal for us. This was a palace in everything but name and its very walls are still impregnated with the earthly glory and the unusual personality of the man who built it. It is spacious and lovely, with the carved chimney breasts, the leaded glass and the ornamentation of the height of the Renaissance. The room whose vaulted ceiling is shaped like the keel of a ship is more perfect in workmanship and more rich in the quality of its wood than the one at Honfleur, but it is no lovelier and is less spontaneous. Above the entrance on the exterior are two simulated windows; from one leans the figure of a woman, from the other that of a man. They call them statues of Jacques Cœur and his wife Macée but I prefer to think of them in their other interpretation, that of two devoted servants set there to await their master's coming. They watched him leave five hundred years ago but, though he never came back, they still stand there waiting for him.

Most of all we loved to return to the cathedral, to its dignity, to its beauty. We went into the interior when the late light vied with flickering yellow tapers, or we studied the elaboration of the great doors until darkness overtook us. But the favorite spot to which our wandering footsteps always carried us was the corner of the old archbishop's garden, with its view of the church. This is now a public park and children play here, chaperoned by their buxom bonnes, or in the evening couples whisper to each other under the trees. It was designed by Le Notre, to whose credit are due many of the well-known gardens of France which, though famous, seem to verdure-loving modern eyes stiff and dry and empty. This one is more gracious than most, the trees are less severely pruned, the grass more plentiful, while the high situation alone would make it beautiful. Its northern side parallels the wall of the church and extends beyond the apse.

When the cathedral was enlarged and the eastern end greatly increased in length, the foundations of this new apse were built beyond the old Gallic Roman wall and into the outer moat surrounding it, so that a good third of this portion is below the normal level of the ground. In other words, one sees the substructure which is usually deep in the soil and hence invisible. The added height increases the feeling of majesty and this mighty apse seems complete enough certainly, sufficiently vast to be a cathedral on its own merits. We looked down at it, across at it, and up to it, and each view increased our knowledge of its beauty. It is so free, it flings its buttresses wide and with such a grand gesture of untrammeled strength and yet, with it all, its design holds together in perfect unity. It is an apse of aspirations in which the spiritual and the artistic are blended in perfect accord.

DIJON

I NEVER cease marveling at human nature. With a world full of interest and with new and exciting things to be seen or done every day, how completely many of us close our eyes and minds to them and think only of the creature comforts. We were in Paris on one of our first pilgrimages, when provincial France was an almost unknown land to us and every step was a discovery. Among other places we were going to Dijon, and the questions we asked of all and sundry received in this case a unanimity of response worthy of a better cause. Even the phrasing was almost identical; " Dijon, ah you have a treat in store for you. How well you will eat there, it is the cuisine of France." That was the stock remark, repeated with variations until we almost changed our plans and omitted this gastronomic paradise from our itinerary. Fortunately we did not, for — though any connoisseurs in such matters may be horrified to realize that our food associations with this famous spot are limited to the recollection of the odd pain d'épice served us in large round cakes and of a peculiarly eggy, oily sauce spilled over me by an untrained waiter, the memory of which seemed to linger through drastic professional cleanings — yet we gained an enrichment of beauty knowledge which has added immeasurably to our mental storehouses.

Dijon is a wide-awake, energetic city, alive to every commercial possibility. It owes its prosperity to the great vineyards which stretch for endless unbroken distances about it and in which ripen the famous grapes which make this one of the wine centers of the world. It is conscious of this position, yet seems curiously blind to its artistic treasures. Seeing Dijon historically is almost a voyage of discovery, so little has that side of it been exploited. I remember endeavoring to find the museum one very warm day. Four times I walked along the street upon which was the entrance, according to my trusty guide book, but only on the fifth passing did I actually find it. This museum is in the old palace of the Dukes of Burgundy and, quite aside from the interesting things it contains, would be notable anywhere for its fine rooms. The old kitchen especially fascinated me. What meals were cooked in this vaulted chamber which now houses only a few sculptures!

The streets are full of unexpected delights, an oriel window or a carved doorway may be found in the most unforeseen quarters. A Renaissance clock tower stands in solitary splendor, the church of which it was originally only a part vanished in the Revolution. A delicate portal and a sculptured staircase are come upon unexpectedly. Even the cathedral of St. Bénigne has the same quality. It is placed so casually, close to the railroad tracks and with no effort at setting or approach. It is perhaps more interesting from the historical than from the artistic standpoint.

St. Bénigne is called a second century saint and martyr, though some authorities place him in the fourth century. He is said to have been born in Greece and sent by St. Polycarp to Gaul, where he spread the gospel of Christianity. He founded a church in Dijon and, following his martyrdom, was buried by his followers in a crypt built to house his sarcophagus, the dimensions of which were said to be enormous. Beneath the fine apse of the cathedral of Dijon is an ancient crypt which was only discovered and restored a hundred years ago. It is simple and primitive and there seems every reason to believe that this and the portions of the tomb which it still contains are those of a sixth century church. It recalls an old miracle. The people worshiped at the so-called sarcophagus of the saint, but Gregory of Langres believed there was a mistake and that their prayers were misdirected. He ordered the practice to cease, then a vision revealed the truth to him and he made public atonement for his doubts, restored the tomb and built a basilica in honor of St. Bénigne, patron of Dijon.

The church of Notre Dame, a most remarkable example of the thirteenth century Burgundian style, is so placed that every view of it is too near for thorough appreciation. Above the triple porch of the façade it is absolutely unique. First there is a band of sculptured ornament from which and above which project figures, human, animal or grotesque. Above them is an arcade of high, slender columns with slightly pointed arches, then another frieze, another gallery and still another frieze. The effect is curious but fine, and how the gargoyle-loving eye longed to draw one of these bands of varied forms! A point of view was impossible, so we resigned ourselves to enjoying them both then and in memory.

There is an ancient Black Virgin in this church, known as Notre Dame du Bon Espoir. For years it was the object of great reverence and devoted love and many miracles were attributed to its power. Then came the Revolution and the overthrow of everything which had been sacred or was a symbol of churchly dominion, at that time so thoroughly feared and hated. The icono-

GARAGE

Saint Bénigne, Dijon, 1929

John Taylor Arms 1927

clastic mob began to invade the churches and wreck the images. A girl, Marthe Launy, wanted to save this sacred Virgin but realized that if her intention were known she would defeat her purpose and probably lose her life as well. She climbed the altar and, grasping the statue, loudly claimed it as her share of the spoils. A man disputed her possession and rudely tore at the coveted prize, knocking down Marthe and dropping the image as well. The Madonna was not seriously injured but the Child was broken into little pieces. As the old records put it, the Son lost His life that His Mother might live.

A cobbler carried the mutilated figure to his home where he kept it many months. Here the curious and the faithful came to see it, paying richly for the privilege. Marthe and her aunt had long been anxious to reclaim the statue, so they gathered together their little hoard of money and bought it secretly from the cobbler, who was beginning to fear persecution by people who envied his new source of revenue. The sale was effected through a third party and the change of habitation took place in the night, with many precautions taken against discovery.

The devout women made a robe for the Virgin as nearly like the old one as their memories and their materials could accomplish. They constructed a little hidden shrine where they might worship unmolested this wonderful and sacred possession. Years passed and when the first wave of religious intolerance had died down pious believers were admitted to the new sanctuary to pray and receive favors. When the church was reconsecrated a few years later, Marthe and her aunt offered the statue which they had so lovingly tended, and the Black Virgin was carried in a procession of great pomp and ceremony and restored to its rightful place in the church of Notre Dame. It is there today, serene and wonder working, only the missing figure of the Child serves as a reminder of those terrible days.

NEVERS

THE rule of three held good for us in Nevers. We had visited it twice before, but it was not until the third time that the exigencies of even casual travel permitted us to tarry long enough for J. T. to make a drawing. The first time was on our way from Avignon to Bourges, when a fortunate discrepancy in train connections gave us two hours or so in which to get a hasty peep at the cathedral and a necessary, if unaesthetic, meal. We toiled up the steep station road between two rows of dreary trees, so pathetically mutilated by indefatigable pruning that they gave no shade whatever and merely suggested brownish-green dusters with most of their feathers gone. It was hot, the streets were empty and the wide squares — white in the sunlight — were empty also. Built on spacious lines, with parks, wide avenues and handsome residences, the town gave a curious suggestion of being an unused place, and this first impression has always persisted in our memories, intensified by subsequent experience. No matter what the time may be, it always seems like the noon hour, or a Sunday. One feels that work and the fretting details of things have been laid aside for a time of relaxation and contemplation. It is a Sleeping Beauty city. The hurrying world of modern commercial life has passed it by and has left it to doze on and dream a bit in a silence made only more complete by the rattle of a solitary cart through the empty, echoing streets.

Yet the inhabitants seemed more than usually prosperous and happy, and they certainly showed an especial amount of consideration and coöperation, as far as an artist and his drawing were concerned. This attitude, by the way, is the finest test I know of the character of a city and it is really extraordinary how true to form each individual in it proves to be. If one person pushes in to see what is happening, knocking things over as he does so, or stands in the light, or gets in front of the subject, then the whole town is much on that same order. The hotel will serve you because it must, but with none of that wonderful air with which some raise their profession to a fine art; the storekeepers will mutter if you go out without buying heavily from them and the children will nudge and stare and giggle at the strangers. In another town (and this is more usually the case) the passer-by will look at the drawing with a soft word of apology for his intrusion, and a gentle " Merci, Monsieur" as he departs, and when that happens one could, I am sure, leave one's most precious possession on the bureau, with perfect confidence in its security, or sit in the center of a crowded street and meet only with friendliness.

The second time we stopped was again on our way to Bourges, this time from Charolles. Again we wanted luncheon, which is always difficult to find in this sleepy spot where the tea-shops close for a day at a time and the cafés serve no omelettes and are out of rolls; and again we visited the church while J. T. made thumb-nail sketches and mental notes of the exact spot where he would place his camp stool Some Day, that visioned moment which so often means No Day! This time Some Day became One Day, and it was with a feeling of accomplishment that we returned yet again.

The cathedral is one of the most curious I know, and, though not at all a perfect example of any architectural style or period, is very interesting and from certain points exquisitely beautiful. The view of it from across the Nièvre, crowning the hill on which it is built, is very dignified and fine, and seen from the east, with its splendid apse and soaring tower, it is quite as lovely. In fact the tower is the focal point and beauty-spot of the city. It is square and high and very Flamboyant in design, and the gargoyles springing from its sides at right angles lend variety to the silhouette without weakening the upward lines. The cathedral is composed of two distinct churches. The Romanesque church of Ste. Julitta, built in the eleventh century, had its main altar and apse at the western end, contrary to the usual custom. The nave was destroyed by fire about a hundred years later, and a second church was added — Gothic in style this time — with another apse and a high altar to the east. The result is that nothing is just where one expects to find it, and there is a lack of central accent and rhythm of design which gives a disturbed feeling. Also, there is no western portal. That rather blank façade is broken by the very low, small apse of the original church, jutting out curiously. One feels that the building has no face, as it were — it appears to be all back and sides.

It seems peculiarly fitting that this dual church, each part distinct in architecture and in feeling, should have been dedicated to a mother and her little son. I wonder if there is a younger saint in the Roman Catholic calendar than this little Saint Cyr, who lived, legend says, at most three short years. Present at the martyrdom of his mother Ste. Julitta, he repulsed the advances made towards him by the Emperor Alexander, even to the point of scratching the imperial face with his tiny nails and proclaiming at the top of his shrill childish voice that he also was a Christian. Finally the emperor, in exasperation, cast him from the elevation upon which he sat, and so he too, poor baby, suffered martyrdom beside his mother.

And here this joint church stands in memory of those two, whose lives had been inseparable for the entire span of one, and who died united by their faith and firm in one supreme, binding thought.

The Gothic end of the church is fine, with some lovely glass in the upper windows of the choir, but I like even better the portion still existing of the Romanesque church at the western end. The transepts, the crypt and the apse remain; the latter, a single chapel with a nearly effaced but most interesting thirteenth century fresco, has no ambulatory. It is raised quite high above the floor of the church and is reached by several wide steps. The arches on either side lead to early Gothic transepts (there are none at the eastern end) and there is a very attractive feature on the south wall. Here a spiral staircase leading to the tower is built partly into the space behind the wall and partly out into the church, with open ascending arches through which one sees the worn stone stairs corkscrewing their upward way until lost to view.

My usual custom is first to study a new church on the outside and then on the inside, with an effort to see it and understand it from a mental point of view. After that I come and go, spending hours or only a few minutes at a time there, with my heart, rather than my mind, open to receive what impressions it may have to give me of its personality, always as marked in a sincere building as in an individual. This double church seemed to me so very poverty-stricken, a little dusty and a little uncared for. I was conscious of more than the usual number of boxes asking for offerings to repair the organ, pay the priests, or keep up the chapels. Spiders had spun many webs between the uprights of the iron grilles, a ladder leaned dejectedly against the masonry wall, with no evidence of any use that had been or was to be made of it, and extra church furniture was stored in thorough confusion in a disused chapel or two. I should certainly have carried away with me a memory none too inspiring, if one day I had not happened to see this shabby church fulfilling its mission in two of its great functions and services to mankind.

In the morning, as I was wandering, I noticed that the door of the stairs leading down to the old crypt under Ste. Julitta's altar was open. I started down, but one glance showed me a low room with sculptured figures encircling it and, in the center, a black-draped coffin guarded by burning candles.

Later in the day, having spent a most interesting hour or two among the examples of faience in the museum, I stopped in again at the cathedral. As I

NÉVERS

THE CATHEDRAL OF ST. CYR AND STE. JULITTA

Size of the original etching, 13 inches by 5⅝ inches

John Taylor Arms 1927

opened the great south door, organ music greeted me and the sounds of violins and voices. A wedding was going on, and, as I had heard of but never really seen this French ceremony, I decided to stay. It was really a lovely sight. They were using the altar at the western end, which, being raised so high above the nave, was both easier to see and especially decorative. The family and intimate friends sat on either side of the chapel and in the middle was the altar, crimson and lace-covered and banked by green plants. The priest stood in the center preaching his sermon, and on either side, sitting in two demure heaps on the altar steps, were little acolytes dressed in scarlet. The bride and groom sat on gilt, red-upholstered seats, their backs to the congregation, her veil carefully draped over the chair back and descending to the floor in a mist of snowy tulle.

The sermon was a long one and quite inaudible to me where I stood, then came the ring ceremony, and after that the two bridesmaids took up the collection! I had heard of this custom but had forgotten about it, and for a moment I could not imagine what they were doing. They came from each side to the altar, received two small baskets duly blessed, then each one, with her attendant groomsman holding her free hand at shoulder-level as if for a minuet, started down the center aisle preceded by a sacristan apiece. I was seized with panic. Was there a fixed sum expected from each spectator, and if so, how could I guess what it was, or would the haughty beadle fix me with a fierce eye and ask me for my card of invitation? I felt uncomfortable and embarrassed, but as the one moment when flight is out of the question is the one when the contribution plate is being passed, I decided to watch my neighbors with an eagle eye and imitate, if possible, their method and amount of giving. As the ribbon-tied basket approached I heard a joyful clink of coins, so I began to feel reasonably sure that a franc would be a safe offering. I dropped one boldly in when my turn came, and then, much to my amusement, the pretty bridesmaid poured part of the contents of her basket into the groomsman's hand, as it was overflowing with massive copper ten centime pieces! I need not have worried about my franc.

Having paid my admission, as it were, I waited to see the couple off in the bridal carriage in which they were to make a tour of the city so that all might see them in their glory. The music pealed forth presently, the priests, fully twelve in number, came down and left the happy couple to make their way out after them as best they might, the more imposing of the two sacristans leading the way for them. Clad in scarlet, with his three-cornered hat of the same color and brave with gold braid, I could hardly believe he was the apologetic, mouselike little man of the morning who had scuttled softly by me in worn felt shoes and a shapeless suit. Such is the power of clothes. His had changed him into this domineering person who, during the contribution, had guarded the lines down which the little basket traveled and who had tapped sternly with his slender silver staff behind two people who had missed contributing, though whether intentionally or not, I do not know. So down the aisle he came, in all the majesty of his clothes and calling, escorting to the sacristy the newly married couple and followed by the bridesmaids and groomsmen, the family and friends. Here, I believe, they were to sign the register and receive congratulations. Soon his assistant, clad less resplendently in black and with heavy silver chains which clanked as he walked, appeared and ascertained that the northern door stood open for the triumphal exit. His red-costumed superior came forth and, with a truly magnificent gesture, rang once — with a mighty clang — the bell on the wall beside him, after which, bearing his staff proudly aloft, he solemnly marched the radiant pair across the nave and out upon the street.

As I turned to leave by the other door, an old man, with the perspiration running off his face and his thin white hair in disorder, was pumping away at the organ in the choir, that it might peal forth the last joyful notes of the recessional, while two old ladies — the typical black-costumed, black-bonneted thin little women who always seem chosen for this particular task — were hastily putting the chairs in order, ready for the funeral which was about to take place. Life and Death, joy and sorrow, so nearly touch.

But Nevers is not just the cathedral, by any manner of means. St. Étienne, to the east of it, is a very ancient and interesting Romanesque church. It was built in the eleventh century and is untouched, except for essential repairs. In style and in execution it is simple to the point of severity, with a plain façade and a very beautiful portal. The lower windows on the sides are narrow and slightly pointed, while the upper ones are hardly wider than archer's slits, and the apse is made up of three simple chapels. One feels the monastic austerity of its origin and the fortresslike solidity of its construction.

On my walk between St. Étienne and the chapel of Ste. Marie (a Renaissance church and not at all to my taste) I had one of the funniest episodes among many. A dear little old lady overtook me and, with confused apologies, asked if I would mind answering a question. Much startled, I naturally replied that I would not, whereupon she inquired where I had bought my shoes! I answered, " In the United States." She sighed and remarked, " That is a long way off. I had hoped they came from Nevers." Then she went on to comment on the comfort of suède shoes and how difficult it was to find them, until I longed to hand over mine. We talked on a bit and she asked about America, saying, with a knowing nod as of one really up on modern things and events, that she had lately been hearing people speak quite often of that country. I thought of our bumptious " Boosters," and how their local and national pride would have suffered from her quite unconscious tone of gentle patronage.

Hurrying back to tell J. T. of my latest adventure, I found a small man, wearing tinted glasses, hovering over him with an expression of anxious solicitude. The sun had come around and was blazing full upon the white paper of the drawing, and this interested spectator (himself an artist) was not alone offering J. T. a sketching umbrella, but was ready to dig up a cobble that the same might be firmly planted in the ground against the wind. Failing that remedy, he was quite insistent that he himself should hold it devotedly and shield the eyes which must look up into that almost unbearable glare.

I never knew a city more full of considerate, lovely people. Even the antique dealer insisted on presenting us with an etching, though our purchases had hardly warranted a bonus, whatever scoffers may say. The final climax came when a priest with a gentle fatherly face came up and asked J. T. if he were making a series of cathedral drawings, and on being informed that this was his aim and intention, " Then," said the priest, " I have a postcard for you. It is addressed ' À Monsieur le Curé de Sainte Julitta et Saint Cyr, pour Monsieur l'Artiste qui fait les dessins des cathédrales de la France.'"

Knowing of old how difficult it is to lunch in France, we brought ours with us when we left Nevers. That remark may sound extraordinary, but I use the word " lunch" advisedly. One may find any number of places, even in quite small towns, where one may dine well on soup or hors d'œuvres, fish or omelette, a hot meat in a heavy, highly seasoned sauce, fruit and cheese, but who could work, or drive, or enjoy the scenery after a meal like that? The two hours which each Frenchman feels an absolute essential at midday, must be largely taken up by the process of digestion, and are certainly requisite. But we, who have learned this, and also that the attractive little shops which advertise tea and chocolate, and have such delectable pastries and breads, all close just at the moment when they would be of use to us — we rely on the trusty tea-basket and a meal provided ahead of time. All of which brings us to Varzy, through which we had hastily passed on our way to Nevers and which we had marked for a visit on our return trip. It may not sound consistent with the enjoyment of architecture to munch a croissant as one contemplates it, but I, personally, have always discovered in myself a better appreciation of any beauty when my fast has not been unduly prolonged. So we parked the car in the open " place" and feasted our eyes upon the very unusual eastern elevation of the church of St. Pierre before us.

The apse is formed by a single chapel terminating in a very high conical roof. Square towers on either side take the place of transepts. These finish in sharply pitched roofs, four-sided this time, while from the eastern face of one a dormered clock keeps time for the little town and from the other an ingenious barometer foretells the weather with almost equal accuracy. Round motives are everywhere used to an unusual extent. The upper portions of the apsidal windows are circular, with four petal-like panes about a smaller central one. Similarly, in the towers, are heavy, deep-set windows with a starlike design, and above, the triple louver-filled arches are surmounted by a round motive of such delicately wrought, intricate tracery that it suggests a stone flower set high in the air.

The western façade is equally interesting and out of the ordinary. The middle portion is narrow and much higher than those fronting the aisles and has a steep-pitched pediment, the tympanum of which shows round penetrations on either side of a central statue. Flying buttresses, pierced by the same circular motive, lend support to the upper part and terminate in heavy piers which rise from the outer walls. These features, and the triple-cusped portal, give an almost Moorish feeling to the whole structure.

We entered through the single weathered doorway and found ourselves in an interior as truly churchly as any I know. It was empty, yet seemed full of a pervading spirit of sheer goodness. The whitewashed walls were pure rather than cold, and in their whiteness a small window gleamed with all the colors of faith and hope, love and truth, joy and sorrow. Outside, the town was quiet as only a Latin town can be at noontime. The bit of street seen through the open portal lay white and dusty under the intense sun, the drone of insects came faintly to our ears and, within and without, the world was at peace.

VÉZELAY

IT is difficult to believe oneself in central France when one contemplates the silhouette and lofty setting of Vézelay, so absolutely do they suggest the hill towns of the south or — to an even stronger degree — those of northern Italy.

It was on a day of high winds and threatening clouds that we wound our way along the valley of the Cure and discovered this, our objective, far in the distance, illumined by a brief moment of brilliant sunshine and framed by the somber lines of nearer hills. It appeared inaccessible on its rudely steep eminence and an unreal thing in the eerie, greenish light which had gleamed out so suddenly between the clouds. A curve of the road lost it to our view; then before long we came to the turning which leads first to the foot of its precipitous hill, then mounting steeper and steeper to the lower town, up through the gateway of St. Étienne, up and up the narrow cobbled street between glimpsed houses — ancient and beautiful, with here a crumbling arch and there a sculptured tower — up and still up to the open " place," and there before us was the Abbey Church of Mary Magdalen.

One of the largest as well as one of the most magnificent of existing Romanesque basilicas, it stands to-day as a monument to man's credulity and his need for expressing his faith in terms of beauty. Heretofore I had always felt that only Gothic could adequately express the spiritual feeling necessary in a church, but this splendid building soon served to disabuse me of this prejudice. It is so strong, so fine, so dignified that it demands and receives unqualified admiration.

My first view of the interior was under rather amusing circumstances. We had arrived in Vézelay at eleven in the morning, a disconcerting hour in the eyes of the residents, as we were too late for breakfast and too early for luncheon. The kindly inn, however, produced an omelette in five minutes, so that noon found us back at the top of the hill and prepared for action, while all the other four hundred and ten inhabitants were eating a leisurely déjeuner. This was all right for J. T., who soon found the exact vantage point he most desired, a spot from which could be seen the fine square tower of the crossing, with the cloisters and a portion of the nave forming a sturdy base and with an ancient well in the foreground to add a bit of human interest. But I roamed about impatiently, eager for the moment when I might enter and see the marvels of which I had heard so much.

Presently the person in charge finished his meal and his wife and baby went for a walk; so, feeling the moment an auspicious one, I approached and asked if I might see the church. To my horror he tore his hair and exclaimed, " What! Now?" in accents of such despair that I felt I must have committed an unforgivable sin. Subsequently I discovered that visitors are supposed to enter in groups, for the great weight of the doors between the nave and narthex makes opening them an effort out of proportion to a single person. Yet opened they must be if one is to get the full beauty of the length of the church.

The *gardien* — who later proved to be of unusual intellectual capacity and fineness of feeling — offered to let me go in alone. I was delighted, so taking up his great keys he solemnly opened a side door and ushered me in, then marched out and closed and double locked the door behind him. I was a prisoner in the midst of unbelievable beauty. J. T. was just outside, but the thick walls were too massive for my voice to reach him and the small, round-arched windows were set too high to be of any use. I resigned myself to my fate, thankful that my temporary captivity was one which offered me so much to see and enjoy. When the clang of an iron key in an iron lock proclaimed my release, I was startled to find how much time had slipped by unnoticed.

The basilica is really a stupendous thing and breath-takingly beautiful. It is one hundred and twenty meters in length, longer even than Notre Dame de Paris we were proudly told. The narthex, one of the largest of its kind, accounts for seventy feet of this dimension and was built thirty years after the completion of the building. Contrary to most Romanesque churches, this one is very high, a fact which quite obviates the heavy, oppressive feeling usual in this style. In fact the daring designers risked defeating their own purpose in so heightening the nave that the vast weight weakened the walls. Only luck and good restoration saved this unique building from destruction.

The side aisles are lower than the central one and more purely Romanesque, while the choir is very ancient Burgundian Gothic. The ornament is still of the earlier style, with round-arched arcades in the chapels, but the arches are slightly pointed and the vaulting has a primitive ribbing.

The color of the interior is very unusual. New stone has been added and much of the old has been scraped to a corresponding pallor, but the actual material varies so much in tone that one gets an idea of how beautiful it must have been in the days before restoration became necessary and when rich fres-

VÉZELAY

THE ABBEY CHURCH OF STE. MADELEINE

Size of the original pencil drawing, 12⅝ inches by 7¼ inches

John Taylor Arms 1919

coes added their brightness. The arches are keyed with blocks of gray and white, which sometimes alternate and sometimes are set apparently according to the taste of the individual workman. Though fainter, they suggest the black and white bands so popular in Siena. In places the stone is a deep, warm yellow, in others richly cream or pale tan. In the north transept there is an area of delicate rosy pink, a glowing note found all through the church in smaller patches, while the deepest color note of all is that of the dark green mould — product of the damp ages — which tints the bases of the piers and parts of the walls and outlines the deep embrasures about the windows.

The most unique feature of the interior lies in its sculptured capitals. No two resemble each other even remotely, yet as one looks down the length of nave or aisle they conform so perfectly to a harmonious, consistent silhouette that one feels the unity of design rather than the great divergence of detail. The range of subject matter is as wide as the treatment. There are capitals on which are represented the Virtues or the Vices next to capitals of pure classical design. There are saints and grotesques, scenes from the Bible and moral lessons whose depiction is crudely vivid. There are scenes of horror and scenes of peace, beauty and ugliness in casual juxtaposition. There are historical incidents and trivial bits of daily life, such as the wine-pressing capital, which surely has no churchly message. Each one is a picture, a story and a marvel.

The beginnings of this church go back so far that they have become legend rather than history; back beyond the time when the Chanson de Geste was sung and told all over this part of France — in the town and perhaps even in the basilica itself — to extol the memory of the founders to whom it owed its first being.

Girard de Rousillon, friend and staunch follower of Charles the Bald, had so many deeds of heroism and loyalty to his credit that the king sent him to Constantinople to interview Jeanne and Berthe — lovely princesses either one of whom might be considered a suitable royal bride. The meeting took place. Berthe was beautiful, clever, charming, but her sister eclipsed her as the sun dims the light of the moon. Girard fell in love with Jeanne, yet loyalty to his sovereign forced him to give an honest report. His eulogies of her charms must have been fervent, for Charles decided on Jeanne and offered Berthe to this faithful follower who loved the king's bride and was loved by her. Poor sister, how unwanted she must have felt. Royal preference carried the day and the lovers parted, exchanging rings which each was to keep as a remembrance and a reminder in case of need. The two marriages were celebrated and, from an inauspicious beginning, long years of marital happiness came to Girard and Berthe, which the ups and downs of a tempestuous life only served to make more precious and more valued.

There were campaigns for the king and campaigns against him. There were angry feuds and rivalries. There were reconciliations which only made the subsequent ruptures more bitter. At length, exiled for many years, Girard determined to try one more expedient. The pair returned to France and, clad as pilgrims, came to the city where were the king and queen. As the latter left mass a roughly clad person accosted her, whom she failed to recognize until he exhibited the ring, her token of their youth. She arranged a meeting with the king and by persuasion and threats finally achieved a peace between them which endured this time.

Tired of war, tired of the intrigues of the world, Girard and Berthe turned their thoughts more and more to religious things. In 865 they founded a Benedictine convent in the valley for their daughter. This was sacked by the Saracens, so, feeling that a more inaccessible location was needed, they built a new one on the heights of Vézelay, changing it to a monastery at this time.

Many stories are told of its building. Berthe, anxious to make an offering which would be more personal, more of a sacrifice than the money they were contributing, decided on a scheme. Girard was away, so every night with one attendant she left secretly and, having secured the aid of a mysterious workman, carried water up the steep hillside to moisten the mortar for the building. An interested friend, whose type is not confined to that long ago time, discovered her secret departures and bore the news to her husband. Disbelieving yet afraid, he returned to spy upon his dearly loved wife and found the story true. But as he watched he saw that the bag of sand which she and her midnight accomplice carried between them was miraculously sustained. Berthe stumbled and dropped the end she held, which yet remained as high from the ground as it had been before. He then knew that spiritual aid had come to her, and joining her they worked together in joyous accord, their labors causing the church to rise with greater speed.

The legend of the saint to whom this great basilica is dedicated is obscure. Mary Magdalen was the sinning woman spoken of in the New Testament as anointing the feet of Jesus. But whether or not she was identical with Mary the sister of Martha, remains in doubt. Some say she went, after the death of the Virgin, to live in Ephesus and died and was buried there. Others that, with Martha and Lazarus, she was put into a rudderless, sail-less boat which was launched on the sea at the mercy of the elements. Due to divine guidance they reached Marseilles in safety, where they went their respective ways. Marie Madeleine — to give her her French name — retired to a bare mountain called that of the Scorpion, where she spent years in repentance. When she died her body was buried at Aix.

Girard wanted the holy relics for his church and one story says that three monks and a prior, inspired by a vision, crossed pagan countries and brought back the sacred body after many and diverse adventures. In this tale some see verification of the story of her death in Ephesus. Another legend says that Badillon was dispatched to Aix, where he and those accompanying him found the town sacked by the Saracens and the chapel destroyed. In momentary danger of their lives they investigated the site of it and discovered a tomb of white marble which exhaled a most exquisite perfume. Sure that they had the right relics, they started on the long homeward journey. On passing a funeral procession one day the corpse of the dead man arose and proclaimed the presence of the saint. Near Vézelay it became impossible to move the body farther, for it had suddenly developed a superhuman weight. Only when the inhabitants of the town and all the clergy had come forth with chanting and flowers, to accompany it joyfully, did the inhibition cease and the body become light enough to be carried to the church.

During the twelfth century the fame of the relics and the miracles performed by them spread increasingly through the land. Vézelay became one of the greatest objectives for pilgrims and the town and the abbey waxed in proportion. Then in the thirteenth century a tomb was discovered in which was found the body of a woman in a perfect state of preservation and with a parchment stating that this was the body of the Magdalen.

Was this a deliberate hoax or was the first one? Or perhaps was it all in good faith? No one knows, or ever will know, but the discovery dealt a death blow to the prestige of Vézelay. The eight hundred monks who had heretofore been none too many to care for the hordes who came in such ceaseless numbers, soon found themselves bereft of their power and of their work. Theirs was once more merely a monastery on a lonely hill, to which the world no longer came. Their prosperity had not proved an unqualified success, they had become domineering and even the feudal lords could not rival their high-handed methods. Once when the Bishop of Autun remonstrated with them he received the curt reply that they considered themselves in his diocese but not of it, an answer calculated to make considerable trouble. There were revolts and uprisings against the monks and their abbot. The abbey, with its precious books and relics, was burned and only a small brotherhood dragged on an undignified existence until the Revolution ended even that.

The town never recovered its prosperity; the streets once gay with life are deserted, the houses put up to receive the busy throngs are falling into decay and of the monks not one remains. The only reminders of this vanished religious life are the vast basilica and, in its shadow, a little school run by gentle nuns. One comes each day to draw a pitcher of water from the well beside the church. Her full black skirts just clear the ground, her voluminous apron is of a deep rich blue, a spotless shawl is crossed beneath her throat and her immense head dress of starched white linen has a tiny gathered crown and long folds which fall demurely on either side of her face. All goes well until a treacherous wind comes up, when she is constrained to hold the flaps close to her cheeks in order to keep her cap and at the same time preserve her dignity.

It is a far cry from this peaceful scene to the days of the twelfth century, when Vézelay was at the height of its popularity. Although miracles are reported, the pilgrims seem to have come chiefly in search of forgiveness. They were of two classes, those who came as a simple act of piety or to expiate some small fault, and those called "public penitents" who, for some grievous sin, had had a severe penance imposed upon them. They were usually commanded to go on foot to St. Jean Compostella — a famous shrine in the Pyrenees — and there perform certain acts of devotion. As the journey was a very difficult and exceedingly dangerous one, it became customary for these penitents to go first to Vézelay, where they began their expiation while waiting for enough other unfortunates to join them to form a group sufficiently strong to set off on the long pilgrimage together.

The lesser sinners were permitted to enter the church and take part in the services. They even might kneel by the high altar and gaze reverently through a narrow aperture cut in the floor, down to the faintly lighted crypt where the holy relics reposed. But the others, the tragic band of public penitents, were outcasts from both religious and earthly contacts. They might not enter the body of the church nor participate in any ceremony. For them the narthex had been built and there they might stand or kneel in lowly penitence, but against them the great doors remained closed — their massive hinges and huge locks a sure protection against any unauthorized opening. Did the beauty and peace of the superb structure to which they were admitted bring them any consolation? I am sure the carved relief in the tympanum, of the Christ with

John Taylor Arms · 1916

arms outstretched above the heads of His apostles, must have been to them a symbol of the mercy and forgiveness they had come so far to seek.

The illusion of being in Italy is intensified rather than diminished as one knows Vézelay better. When we toiled up the central street, or slipped precariously on its cobblestones as we descended, even this steepness served to accentuate the similarity. Old houses, many of them deserted and partly in ruins, crowded out over the sidewalk in a manner truly Italian and the vistas down narrow streets showed fertile plains and distant hills of a Lombardy blueness.

We walked one evening of glowing light up an inviting way and found ourselves upon the grassy road which encircles the town at the base of the old walls. These rose on our right, masked by ancient ivy with trunks the size of trees. On the left we looked down from our hillside across the plain to slopes patterned by fields and vineyards and bathed in a radiance suggestive of warmer lands. A little farther on a flight of stairs, built out from the wall and protected by a slender balustrade of wrought iron, led up to the door of a house far above our heads. Mighty trees formed a cathedral aisle of green, limes and walnuts and chestnuts. The old fortified gate came into view, two round towers from the sides of which an occasional stone projected curiously.

From around the curve before us came a flock of newly shorn sheep, who hurried from spot to spot nibbling frantically as if their very lives depended upon each last furtive bite. Behind them a ferocious dog advanced towards us with menacing growls. His master spoke to him and he moved on reluctantly, looking back at us with considerable distrust. From the same lack of confidence in him I, too, kept a wary eye over my shoulder, and so saw a girl who had been picking wild flowers on the bank join the young shepherd. When I last saw them they were walking arm in arm towards the glowing west, the fat sheep ably marshaled before them by their canine guardian.

We walked on, our way always ascending and later curving sharply to the right. We came to a division of roads; one grassy track led on around the hill and down the other side where the gardens are, the other turning led us up the hill to the wide terrace behind the church. This was the site of the old abbey and the garden where the monks sat in the sun or walked for recreation. Only a few stone seats and some ruined steps are left, but the glorious trees and the view from the surrounding wall are as beautiful now as then. From here one looks out over the valley, where the windings of the Cure may best be traced by following the lines of trees upon its banks, down to a town of red-tiled roofs and away off to the distant, luminous hills.

The spell of Vézelay grows on one with time. I spent long happy hours in the shadow of the wall over against the church, with J. T. drawing busily beside me and hurrying clouds forming changing patterns of brilliant shadow on the masonry before me. The church has weathered to a brownish gray, full of warmth and light, while here and there on sheltered surfaces orange lichen has patched it with intense color. The square tower is deeply gray, its upper structure so time-tinted that the alternating bands of light and dark stone are barely discernible save as a slight variation of tone.

I watched the shadows lengthen from short, crisp replicas of the overhanging eaves to luminous bands cast by the sturdy buttresses which ably brace the lateral aisles. I watched the light change from a hard glare to a pearly glow in which each color became both deeper and softer and the great building turned rosy in the setting sun, seeming to shine with an inner radiance.

Then it appeared to me once more as the church of the pilgrims, the wonder-working shrine to which came so many sorrowing, sinning people for expiation and repentance, and which gave them such abundant forgiveness and comfort.

TROYES

WHEN I think of Troyes it is with a feeling of perpetual wonderment that this interesting city is not more widely known. Quite traveled foreigners have usually never heard of it, and only the most inveterate French tourist knows it by more than name. Yet it is rich in beauty and history to an extent quite out of proportion to its size or reputation. It has any number of narrow streets lined by half-timbered houses with lowering gables and quaint dormers; it has remnants of Renaissance architecture as lovely as any to be found outside of Touraine; it has fourteen churches of intense interest, ten of them "Monuments Historiques," and it has a crowning glory in the wealth of its stained glass.

According to old records and paintings, the Troyes of the seventeenth century was a place of churches and belfries. What a babel of sound there must have been when the noon hour was sounded by one hundred and twenty-six clocks, more noisy even than the modern siren which seems to have taken possession of industrial France and which is no exception here. History says that the clamor of these bells gave rise to many recriminations and lawsuits between neighboring churches, when the chimes of one seriously interfered with the service or sermon going on in another. It also started the old saying "You come from Troyes, what are they doing there?" "They are ringing."

A busy, noisy place it must have been in those days of old, with clock towers clanging forth each quarter hour from above and in the streets below shrill-voiced, chattering crowds doing business at the great "foires" or open markets. The custom of gathering merchandise of all kinds and selling it thus on the streets of Troyes is said to have been the origin of all the foires of modern-day France; so famous did they become and so thoroughly did they set a standard for excellence of goods and honesty of measure, that the expression "Troy Weight" is supposed to be derived therefrom. People came from far and near to sell, to buy and to exchange, and the prosperity which this great commerce brought about lasted for many years.

It is still a commercial city, though the wares and the methods of sale have radically changed. In the middle ages the streets were once crowded with open stalls to such an extent that special churches were constructed to fulfill the religious needs of the transient merchants. St. Jean au Marché and St. Rémi were the principal ones, and portions of the original buildings still exist. St. Jean has been sadly altered by time and man, but the apse is still lovely and the quaint belfry lends it a gay and festive air. Upon a wide and solid foundation tower, where hangs one small bell rung for the celebration of mass, is built a small, rectangular, flat-topped turret which supports three more bells — a large one to strike the hours, another very much smaller for the half hours and a third, still smaller, for the quarters. Quite an imposing array for a single edifice. Henry the Fifth of England was married to Katherine of France in this church, or in the cathedral — there seems to be a divergence of opinion on this point. The union of King Hal and his " bonny Kate" brought trouble to the land and long wars which only the successful campaigns of Jeanne d'Arc terminated.

The great commerce of olden times was in linen sheets, cotton materials and leathers. Now it is a city given over to the making of " bonneterie," that odd French word which most foreigners find confusing. During my early days of foreign shopping I found myself in one of the huge department stores of Paris, where, among other errands, I was to buy a cap for a young child. Great signs hung everywhere above the milling crowds of bargain hunters and in the distance one marked " Bonneterie" in enormous letters seemed a very beacon to lead me to the section where I would be. So, confidently, I turned my steps in that direction, only to find myself in a wilderness of hosiery and knitted things! Modern Troyes has up-to-date stores where stockings and their like abound and the old markets have disappeared; now there is only a covered iron one whose hideous practicality houses perishable foodstuffs.

Henry I, Count of Champagne, was a great believer in these old fairs and did everything to extend and encourage them, for which commercial astuteness and other progressive traits his grateful people named him the Liberal. He also was responsible for the canals which make waterways all through the town and which must have added greatly to its efficiency, as they add now to its attractiveness. Troyes — like Paris — was built on an island in the Seine and as it outgrew its first narrow confines it found itself crowded on to marshy banks and subject to disastrous floods. The construction of canals diverted the water into proper channels, drained the wet land on either side and formed a perfect means of transporting to all parts of France the local goods produced in such quantities. In some sections these are now vaulted over and one only guesses at the current flowing ceaselessly beneath an otherwise commonplace street. In others, they are open and reflect on their tranquil surfaces the houses lining their banks. They are spanned by little bridges which are only wide enough for a single cart or car and which occasionally open to permit the passage of some laden barge.

Near one of these canals — wide enough to be dignified by the name of Basin — is the church of St. Urbain. The story of its building is as strange as any fiction. In 1185 there was born to a poor shoemaker of Troyes a boy whose name was Jacques Pantaléon, marked from birth for an ecclesiastical career. He started as a choir boy in the cathedral, then studied and became a priest and received one honor and advancement after another until, in 1261, he ascended the papal throne as Urban IV. He was Pope for only three years, but during that short time he accomplished two things; the establishment of the Fête Dieu, perhaps the most beloved and widespread of all feast days in France, and the endowment and commencement of this very exquisite church. He dedicated it to his patron saint and built it in loving, understanding memory of his own humble origin, with the sanctuary above the exact site of his father's house. He did not live to see the result of his vision. Driven from place to place by the opposing forces of Manfred, he died virtually in exile and perhaps poisoned, leaving the work to be carried on by his nephew, Cardinal Ancher. The latter did not have an altogether easy time of it. The construction was only just thoroughly under way when difficulties arose. The ground on which it was being built belonged to a nearby convent of great wealth and influence. Why an otherwise far-seeing Pope should not have taken this fact into consideration, I do not know, but at any rate the abbess (who must have been a woman of temper quite inconsistent with her vows) took umbrage at this invasion of her territorial rights. One fine day, with her devoted nuns and her sympathetic adherents behind her, she marched into the partially built church and ordered the workmen away; then, with a right good will, they knocked over stones and demolished the structure as best they could. It must have been quite a sight to see these belligerent women intent upon their errand of destruction, with their demure habits kilted up for freer action and their faces aflame with the light of fury quite at variance with their habitual expression of sweetness. Another similar episode occurred the following year when the Bishop of Auxerre — who had come to Troyes to officiate at the benediction of the cemetery — had his ears soundly boxed by the same recalcitrant abbess. He promptly — and I feel with reason — excommunicated the irate lady and her band of nuns and so the work went on in peace until a little later one of the many fires which have so often ravaged this city brought about another interruption. In 1286 — about fourteen years after the first stone was laid — all work on it ceased and it was nearly a century later before a temporary wooden roof and west wall were built, closing in the church sufficiently to permit of its consecration. Houses grew up about the unfinished sides and it was to this concealment that it owed its escape from mutilating or restoring hands. It was not until 1875 that the work of construction was carried on, as nearly as possible in accordance with the original design. So it is in consequence a very pure, a very consistent example of a brief period of architectural style, a fact which makes it of great interest.

The nave is short, giving the effect of a building almost square; the proportions are very fine and the detail quite unusual. The small windows of the nave disappear behind and above the vaulting and the windows of the apsidal chapels have an extra, rather heavy, stone tracery in front of them. Seen in direct elevation this tracery gives depth of vision and color, but from an angle it cuts into the pattern of the glass. Although three centuries before the first Flamboyant Gothic made its appearance, this thirteenth century church shows many of its forms and tendencies. A proof, I suppose, of the fact that each style is a perfectly consistent outgrowth of the preceding one. The shallow, thin porches added so recently seem insufficient and are particularly out of scale in their juxtaposition with the very heavy, massive buttresses which surround them. But here, as in every other church in Troyes, the painted glass is remarkable in design, color and imagery.

Nearby is Ste. Madeleine, a treasure also and with an exquisite rood screen of which they tell a human, interesting tale. The sculptor, Giovanni Gualdo, had competed for the great portals of the cathedral, but to those who have seen the transepts of Beauvais and of Sens it is unnecessary to add the information that Martin Chambiges won, and Gualdo lost, this competition. The latter — hurt in his local pride, for was he not of Troyes, and hurt in his personal egotism, for was he not known as the master mason? — put into the rood screen which he was then designing for Ste. Madeleine all the accumulated energy of wounded vanity and unfulfilled ambition. They say that his aim was to make this work so beautiful that not only the committee which had refused his design but also his fellow townsmen would regret bitterly the unloyal choice which had brought in an alien artist. If that really was his intention I think he almost, if not quite, succeeded. The portals of St. Pierre and St. Paul are very beautiful, and the sculptures before their destruction during

John Taylor Arms 1918

the Revolution must have been free, rhythmic and structural, but in wealth of detail, in exquisiteness of form, in the loving artistry which lavishes supreme thought and skill on the most insignificant surface, they cannot approach Gualdo's achievement. When it was completed he said that he would cheerfully await the Day of Judgment beneath it without any fear of being crushed. His faith has been justified so far, his masterpiece stands there intact and solid and, by a freak of justice, for many years his body rested beneath it as he had wished.

Troyes proved the exception to a usually unvarying family tradition. It demonstrated that a superb subject and good working conditions can be found together, however rare the occurrence may be. In Troyes the always possible exception obtained. The lovely apse is best seen from a quiet adjoining court; a kindly concierge permitted us to make ourselves at home there, always providing that we did not mind being unable to leave between the hours of twelve and two, when she locked the gates for the usual period of time needed for a French déjeuner. So before noon I would hurry in, laden with tiny packages — two " petits pains " from the boulangerie in one, two pastries from the patisserie in another and, from the fruitier, juicy apricots in a little bag. So thoroughly do the French shops specialize that it was impossible to buy all of even such a simple al fresco meal in any one store. Happily shut in, with the tea kettle cozily boiling, we lunched in undisturbed tranquillity.

In the morning the sun cast long shadows across the court, at noon we watched the line creep nearer and nearer and speculated as to whether or not it would reach the drawing board and make a glaring whiteness of it so hard on the eyes, and in the evening the shade from the great trees — horse chestnut, plane tree and mimosa — reached over to us with grateful coolness and the air was sweet from the heat-drenched blossoms over our heads. At midday the bell in the tower tolled its appointed twelve strokes with slow resounding dignity, while the siren competed raucously with it; the old and the new were in almost comical contrast. The hum of the city came faintly to our ears, a child in a nearby house cried or sang according to its mood, the pigeons cooed from their inharmonious dovecote built casually above the cathedral eaves, and a flock of irritable geese honked from an inner courtyard. All was peaceful detachment, with only the incongruous click of a typewriter from an office building in the corner to remind us of a businesslike and humdrum world.

From this quiet court I made my pilgrimages to the cathedral. From summer heat I passed with a few short steps into the chill of the vast interior.

This contrast of temperature seemed an echo of the same quality in the building. It was originally built in the thirteenth and fourteenth centuries and consecrated in the presence of Jeanne d'Arc and Charles VII. Then there were changes and reconstructions, due to fires or to the settling of the ground on the south which threatened the entire edifice. It embodies in its structure features of almost every Gothic style and period, yet the resulting whole is surprisingly harmonious. The great façade is highly worked and finely sculptured, while the interior is almost severely plain. The first piers of the nave are as large as any I have seen and the others are very massive, but the general effect is of lightness. The lowness of the nave is supposed to keep the interior from ranking with the greatest of Gothic churches, yet I felt, on entering it, soaring, aspiring height. This is brought about, I suppose, by the high windows of the clerestory above the graceful arcade of the triforium, behind the arches of which is another line of brightly colored windows. The style of the interior is very simple, with plain chapels and a refreshing absence of polychrome statues; and so beautiful is the glass, and in such abundance, that one feels a richness of furnishing rather than a lack of it.

To Troyes, more almost than to any other one city, belongs the honor of bringing stained glass to a high degree of perfection and beauty and over a great number of years. Each one of the ten churches which the government has set aside as " Monuments Historiques" has examples of this beautiful art, but the cathedral has — not alone the greatest quantity — but an almost unbroken series, representing every epoch and every style of development. It is like a specialized museum where one may look and study at one's leisure and under the most perfect conditions.

The great rose to the west is hidden by a hideous organ loft, so that one may see it only from the choir. It has an unusual background of clear yellow, and the late light through it is golden. The older windows have generally very small designs and are made up of tiny bits of glass. The legend of St. Loup, Bishop of Troyes, depicted in the choir, recalls his famous battle with Attila in the fifth century. The barbarian hosts were pressing hard about the city and St. Loup called down from the fortified walls to their commander and asked whom he might be. The answer came back, " The flail of God." ".Oh," said St. Loup, " And I am the most miserable of God's creatures; I must be beaten by His flail," and hastening down he opened the gates to the besieging forces. Divine intercession blinded them and they could see nothing but empty streets, so they hurried through the city without touching it and were annihilated a little later by other forces who believed more in the principle of being helped if they helped themselves.

Another window in the north aisle is very curious. It is called the Mysterious Wine Press and suggests a Tree of Jesse. At the base is a figure, perhaps that of Christ, lying in a press and from His side springs a large vine which flowers into bishops and other prelates of the church, each bearing a bunch of grapes.

Our court was locked at six each day, so with an hour or two of daylight still at our command we explored the quaint streets and ancient churches, one by one. Troyes is more replete with a wealth of interest than any other city I know in provincial France, with the exception of Rouen. The old quarter of half-timbered houses is almost as large and quite as ancient, though perhaps the individual examples are less varied and less beautiful. The Rue des Chats is the narrowest and the quaintest of all. Six feet at its widest, the eaves of the houses on one side of the street literally overlap those on the other side, and farther on the upper stories of two are joined into a tiny bridge. The section around Ste. Madeleine and St. Jean is particularly full of this type of mediaeval architecture and has, besides, lovely examples of lordly residences, built at the time of the Renaissance.

Beyond the cathedral we found St. Nizier, an old church with a Gothic nave and apse and a crumbling Renaissance façade. It has a curious sanctuary, the apsidal chapels of which are shallow and almost flat.

St. Rémi has a lovable, lived-in quality ; we felt it was a church to which people went spontaneously, one which formed a very real part of their daily lives. The apse was haphazard, with chapels projecting aimlessly and buttresses of no apparent function raising their heads among the confused lines of roofing. It looked as if construction had been interrupted just before a harmonious end had been attained. The south portal had a little lodgelike house, built comfortably against its protecting wall, the conciergerie I suppose. Bright flowers in pots decked the window sills and a green canary in his great gilt cage sang as if to compete in tone with the gaiety of their colors. All around its weathered sides the market held full sway, and as we passed through the simple crumbling door, the voices of merchant and purchaser alike came to us as a busy hum.

The inevitable moment of departure came one afternoon and we left our quiet retreat and walked around to the western end of the cathedral for a farewell memory. We looked through the great open portals, up the dim nave to the choir windows. The strong sunshine in which we stood filtered through them, bereft of its red and yellow tones. We saw a pattern of light of an inde-scribable celestial blue, which was neither the color of mid-ocean nor that of the sky at night, yet something of both; a light so pure, so spiritual that it seemed a beacon illuminating the way to heaven.

SENS

THIS world, made up of human units as it is, is an egotistical place and the trait shows itself in nations, in organizations and in individuals. Why it should matter greatly to anyone that he, or his town, or his country should own the largest, or the smallest, or the oldest, or the newest something-or-other, is a mystery; yet in reality this is one of the most potent factors in life. An innocent but characteristic example of it is the local pride evinced by every true Frenchman who — however small or unimportant his church — invariably confides in one that, though Chartres, Amiens, Rheims, are of course great cathedrals, yet, Madame, in its way ours has such and such merit and is, in the opinion of those who know, unique!

On a short side street in Sens, where J. T. had settled himself to draw, a little comedy was enacted exemplifying this proprietary pride. Two savants in long, tight-fitting black coats paced back and forth, their heads bent, their hands clasped behind them, their pointed beards truculently wagging as they talked. One was from Beauvais, the other a local man, and their argument was as to the relative merits of the southern transept of the cathedral of one and the northern transept of that of the other. The latter towered untroubled above them as they walked and talked. The burden of their refrain was thus, " But after all, Monsieur, it is admitted by those who know that my church is the finer."

There was good ground for this discussion. The resemblance between these portions of the two cathedrals is so startling that we were not surprised to find that Martin Chambiges designed them both. In spite of local chauvinism, Beauvais is the greater achievement; one feels in Sens a little repetition, a little less of the exuberant vitality and enthusiasm of the other design, and one remembers the bitter jealousy and heart burnings of the two cities over this famous Parisian architect of the fifteenth century. Both places wanted to have him all the time and, that being an obvious impossibility, they resorted to make-shifts and various subterfuges to keep him beyond his appointed stay. Once Chambiges was held a virtual prisoner in Beauvais, a fact which perhaps accounts for the greater detail of that transept — a result of unquestioned beauty though the method of obtaining it was hardly of the same quality. Does the end ever justify the means?

The general effect of the Cathedral of Sens is fine, though the massive western end, in spite of many beautiful features, is unsatisfactory. This is largely due to structural weakness. In the original building the façade was considerably lower and two towers were planned to rise from either end. In 1268 the southern one fell and it was found necessary to strengthen the wall. This was done by building it much higher, so that, as we see it to-day, it hides the ridge of the great roof and is joined to the never completed northern tower for more than half its height, and to the southern one for its entire elevation. So it seems a façade too high for its width and the soaring spires of the design are reduced now to mere flanking buttresses. The one to the right does rise above the rest of the church, yet its height is abortive and one loses its real beauty of proportion and detail in its too long connection with the west wall beside it. The small turret crowning it is set daringly off axis. It is a gay little candle-snuffer affair, but as completely misplaced as a rakish hat over a serious, heavy face.

Built in the early part of the twelfth century, on the site of a basilica which had in turn succeeded two others before it, St. Étienne of Sens ranks as the oldest Gothic cathedral in France. It is believed that a few small churches had already used the vaulted nave and Suger is known to have employed the same style in the choir of St. Denis, but this was the first attempt to roof the nave of any large building in this manner. So that the claim of Sens Cathedral to priority in this matter of architectural structure seems to be better established than those of other churches for particular characteristics.

The interior of the cathedral gives an impression of great purity, which detailed subsequent study does not support. This effect is largely obtained by the harmonious nave, which is formed of alternating clustered pillars and twin engaged columns, and by the lovely gray of the stone of which it is built. The stained glass in the northern side of the choir is very beautiful and quite unusual and the design of each window is geometric, so much so that one wonders if the cubist movement is very new after all. One window depicts the life of Thomas à Becket who, during his exile from England, lived in Sens and was its archbishop. Bits of his vestments can still be seen in the Treasury. His residence here had one interesting and rather unexpected result. When he returned to his native land he took with him William, an architect of Sens but not the designer of the cathedral, as has often been erroneously stated. Saturated with the beauty of his church, William rebuilt the recently burned Cathedral of Canterbury on the lines and of the type of this one. He used as much of the remaining edifice as possible and cleverly incorporated the new style into it, with the result that Canterbury is curiously reminiscent of Sens.

A statue of Thomas à Becket, which came from the house he occupied in Sens, is in the ambulatory. During the Revolution it was hidden under a thick coating of mortar to prevent its destruction. The only other statue to escape the religious vandals is that beautiful one of St. Stephen on the dividing pillar of the main portal; the words " La Loi" on his Bible were the means of sparing him his head.

The central apsidal chapel, with a quite terrible eighteenth century stucco group, has a fine window commemorating the life and martyrdom of St. Savinian. Being rather a local saint, one often finds monuments to him here. He and his half-sister Savine were children of a pagan named Savin, who became very angry when his son, having read the verse " Asperges me Domine," refused to rest until he knew its meaning and refused also to sacrifice to the gods of his people. One night Savinian had a vision and left home secretly, coming to Troyes where he was baptized in the Seine and where he converted many people to Christianity. The emperor Aurelian, enraged by his power, attempted to have him tortured and killed but with no success. The flames would not burn him and the arrows aimed at his heart remained suspended in mid-air. When this occurred the emperor, in great anger, came and mocked him; whereupon one of the hanging arrows turned and, driving itself into his eye, blinded him. Later, knowing that death was imminent, the saint prayed that he might meet it at the place of his baptism; his prison was miraculously opened and he walked to the spot beside the river where he wished to be, and there — after telling his executioners that a drop of his blood applied to Aurelian's eye would restore his vision — he was decapitated. He then walked forty-nine paces with his head in his hands.

But the transepts are the beauty spots of the whole church. One reaches the southern — less ornate and a little smaller than the other — through the loveliest sixteenth century sculptured doorway, set incongruously in a modern wall, and through a courtlike garden of growing green and elaborate wrought iron railings. The north portal is more massive and the design and execution are more perfect. Pillars of intricate Gothic motives flank it on either side and the carving is lacelike and profuse. The very high, very beautiful roofs of the church — of tiny, moss-grown slates — form an interesting background for its delicacy. It was while making this drawing that J. T. had an amusing experience. Two men — one holding a small boy by the hand — had stopped to look on, and when a Frenchman looks he usually talks also. So, no exception to this rule, they made their compliments; one remarked it took time; the other agreed and added that it took patience; the first assented and said feelingly that it took courage. Then the child's voice contributed that it also took " knowing how." J. T. was both amused and pleased; the father patted the youngster on the head, proclaiming him an " enfant précoce," and with mutual felicitations they went their separate ways.

From the gallery above the west façade, as well as from the south tower, there is a splendid view of the hilly, fertile country round about the crowded town, and of the beautiful roofs of the cathedral. I spent quite a while up there, getting a little perspective on things. It was easier to visualize the old shape of the church when looking down on the obviously more recent high transepts, and the reason for the strengthening wall between the towers became very apparent. The ornament is surprisingly delicate, considering the height at which it is placed, and is profuse and varied. There are sculptures which cannot possibly be seen from below; a love of beauty that counted not the labor involved must have prompted their chiseling. I was studying some of the details with considerable interest when one bit, curiously placed and darker than the surrounding stone, caught my eye. It projected from the angle where a narrow, shelving ledge joined the wall and it looked like a face half obliterated by time and the elements. I had about decided that it was some freak of design similar to the tiny head which peeps out at one from the clustered columns of the nave below, when it moved and flew away. My ancient sculpture was merely a very quiet modern pigeon!

To the east I noticed the church of St. Jean, now in the grounds of the Civil and Military Hospital, with a lovely and very old chapel; and St. Savinian with a tower said to be of the eleventh to thirteenth centuries, though from a nearer inspection I should say that it must have been drastically restored. St. Pierre le Rond, to the west, has another belfry so characteristic of the Burgundian Gothic of this section. It is a square tower; the upper portion where the bells hang has the inevitable very large, very projecting louvers, and the whole is surmounted by a slated cupola almost mosquelike in shape.

This church is in the old section of the town, the part where one can visualize a little the forms and customs of mediaeval times. One looks down into it as into a toy village and in truth it seems as artificial, with its high-peaked roofs grown soft with the moss of ages, its half-timbered fronts bulging with the weight of years and its quaint dormers in sharp silhouette. It was when all

North Portal, Sens.

John Taylor Arms 1919

the city looked like this that Mme. de Miramion came to the end of her curious adventure here — a tale as strange and incredible as the plot of a modern movie.

She was a widow of twenty, beautiful and rich but with a serious mind and a definite trend towards a religious life. She had dearly loved the young husband who died a few months after their marriage and all idea of a successor to him was repugnant to her. Many aspirants endeavored to make her change her mind, but without avail; more and more did she feel inclined to withdraw herself from the world.

The villain of the piece then appeared, Count Bussy-Rabutin, cousin of Mme. de Sévigné and at one time suitor for her hand. He found himself widowed, the father of three daughters and heavily in debt. The wealthy widow seemed the ideal way out of his difficulties and, having a turn for the dramatic, he went about his wooing in rather singular fashion. Perhaps his vanity could not bear the thought of another refusal which would be bruited about in his social set, always eager for bits of gossip and preferably for news derogatory to one who stood none too high in court favor. Whatever his reasons, he approached the matter circumspectly. He got into communication with the father confessor of the lady in question, who arranged for him to see and judge of her charms for himself. This priest — an unscrupulous person — divulged, for a consideration, the totally false knowledge that she also had seen the Count, was impressed by his appearance and was only too glad to consider the match, but that her family held different views and would never permit it.

A little later, as the unsuspecting lady was driving home from an evening service, her carriage was set upon in St. Cloud by a band of armed men. Her escort was overpowered, her ceaseless shrieks brought no aid and she was carried off, clinging to one companion with the strength born of desperation. There was a moment's hope when the carriage stopped to change horses. Her screams attracted attention, which was soon diverted by the statement that she was an insane woman being taken to necessary isolation. Her chance was gone and they galloped on through the night. Presently they reached the Château de Launay where, seizing two loaded pistols from a nearby table, Mme. de Miramion prepared to make a last brave stand.

Her gentlemen abductors were frankly puzzled. They had expected a willing captive, whose cries would be merely the proper expression of shy womanhood; whereas they had on their hands a struggling wild thing whose piercing, unceasing lamentations rang strangely true. They disclosed the plot

[165]

and found, to their intense consternation, that she was totally ignorant of it. Here was a pretty situation! Bussy-Rabutin appeared and implored her to marry him, if only to save her own honor, but she remained obdurate. Finally, swearing with uplifted hand that she would never consent, she fainted from sheer exhaustion. Things were desperate. They were convinced she meant what she said, and the sooner they got rid of her, the better for everyone. Her carriage was called and she was driven to the gates of Sens, where she was forced to descend and make her way in, on foot and alone. She had great difficulty gaining an entrance through the fortified gates, closed through the night, and when she finally succeeded it was only a wraith of herself which reached the inn. She lay there for weeks, desperately ill and tenderly cared for by the sympathetic inhabitants. The bishop brought her spiritual comfort and offered his aid to her brother de Rubelle, who had come to avenge the kidnaping.

The thing dragged out into a long lawsuit. Mme. de Miramion subsequently forgave her abductor and later founded in Paris a famous order of women who devoted their lives to good works, yet took no formal vows. She passed away regretted by all, a woman whose memory still lives as a constructive force; while Bussy-Rabutin died as he had lived, unloved, unregretted, still in debt and still a widower.

AUXERRE

SOMETIMES only a few kilometers separate one town from another, yet the difference in the spirit and personality is so vast that a continent might lie between them.

We left Sens — a busy place of factories and street fairs, but a place where business was done by the French and for the French, and where the traveler was one to be courteously treated and not exploited for financial profit — and in a little while we were in Auxerre, a tourist-ridden city of professional courtesy and hurried, half-hearted interest. Even the streets are posted with tidy signs on the corners, " Au Vieux Auxerre," " À la Cathédrale," " Au Musée." One church is actually marked with the name and date of its construction. Yet, in spite of this ticketed condition, there is here such a quantity of architecture, history, quaint streets and beauty of color, that one soon forgets the other side.

There is a picture at every turning, and there are more turnings than straight ways in this town built upon angular twin hills. Before our luggage was unloaded we went exploring, plunging down the steep, perilously narrow streets in momentary danger of losing a mudguard, so absorbed were we in gazing to right and left at such a wealth of beauty. It might be an old house with dormers like beetling eyebrows, or a vivid garden glimpsed through an open door, or the cathedral itself rising majestically above a serried mass of red-tiled roofs — each picture was lovelier than the last and we finally emerged on the quays breathless from too much looking.

The finest views were to be found on the other side of the river. In the foreground, the green Yonne flowed gently by. Barges were moored to its banks, or moved with a kind of heavy dignity. Beyond, the town rose abruptly, with the cathedral on one hill, the church of St. Germain on the other and a sharply dipping little valley between. This latter church is only a fragment, but ancient beyond belief even in this country of antiquity. It goes back to the fifth century and to Clothilde, Christian wife of Clovis, the pagan king. She gave birth to a son whom she caused to be baptized, with the rather unwilling consent of his father. When the child died shortly afterwards his reproaches were bitter, but she replied that it was an honor for their first-born to be called to a celestial realm ; it would be time enough for the second to rule over a terrestrial kingdom. The second boy was born, christened, and then he too fell ill. Black was the king's despair but, fortunately for the cause of Christianity, the child recovered and later Clovis was converted and baptized by St. Rémi at Rheims.

This steadfast queen, who did so much to aid the growth of the new religion, little realized that later she herself would be canonized. Appreciating the goodness and constructive life of Germain, bishop of Auxerre, she built in his honor this abbey church in which he lies buried. Only part of it remains. The great choir and transepts rise above the surrounding houses, their height accentuated by the steep pitch of the hill. Beyond is the isolated tower, separated from them by the space once occupied by the nave of the original church. This tower is Romanesque, tall, slender, gray, austere yet delicate. It seemed hauntingly familiar and we realized that weak, ghostly copies of it were raised beside almost every church built in our own country at the end of the nineteenth century, when a wave of that particular style inundated the land.

A *gardienne*, living in the base of it, gave us an immense key, also orders as to the turning on and off of lights. We joyously went on alone into this fragment of a mighty church, still beautiful in spite of whitewashed walls and the dusty emptiness of a disused sanctuary. A few steps brought us down into a crypt of low, primitive vaulting and intricate plan. It suggested the catacombs of Rome, with its inner rooms opening out unexpectedly, its walls with tiers from floor to ceiling, in the recesses of which repose tombs containing the earthly remains of bishops and sainted men, and its early, half-obliterated frescoes.

There were curious little chambers, of which two walls were solid, two with the simplest piers and arches. Definite information as to their use was lacking, but they were thought to be intended to contain some particularly honored sarcophagi. There were columns with capitals positively Egyptian in feeling, and there was a recently uncovered mural, the graceful design of which made us particularly regret the missing portions. In one or two places our footsteps echoed hollowly. Investigation by the aid of an anachronistic but useful electric bulb on a long cord, revealed an iron ring which lifted a slab and disclosed two tombs in the cavern below, their stone covers carved from end to end and from side to side with the simple, sturdy cross of the Merovingians.

Due to the conformation of the ground, the inner portion of the crypt is deep in the rock and soil of the hill, while the high masonry walls of the outer part are far above the level of the earth. From an apsidal chapel containing a fireplace, small slits of windows, fortresslike in their narrowness, offered us

AUXERRE

CHURCH OF ST. GERMAIN, SEEN FROM THE YONNE

Size of the original pencil drawing, 10¾ inches by 16½ inches

AUXERRE
CHURCH OF ST. GERMAIN, SEEN FROM THE YONNE
Size of the original pencil drawing, 10½ inches by 10½ inches

tantalizing glimpses of a magnificent view over town and river to the gently rolling countryside beyond. Yet so steep is the incline of the hill that only a short distance away, at the end of a brief aisle, we stooped to pass under a low arch and found ourselves in a black space into which no light penetrated. We groped about with tentative steps and outstretched arms, and knew by touch only that we were in a rude chamber whose walls were cut out of the living rock.

In the center of the crypt is the tomb of the saint for whom the church was built, and to whom was due much of the rapid growth of Christianity during the fifth century. His life was one of contradictions, a man who carried the force of his character and his boundless energy, first into his worldly life, and later into his spiritual one.

Young, frivolous, debonair, he yet made a good and just governor of the duchy of Burgundy. His careless, pleasure-loving ways were as a thorn in the flesh to Amador, bishop of that diocese. Especially did his love of the chase anger this worthy prelate, who preached and exhorted in vain, until finally, goaded beyond prudence, he cut down the tree on which Germain loved to hang the trophies of his hunting. This precipitated a storm from which Amador wisely fled, then returned secretly, inspired by a vision. He lured the unsuspecting governor to the cathedral, tonsured his hair by force, and foretold that Germain would succeed him as bishop of Auxerre. I do not imagine that this prophecy was received in a coöperative spirit, yet in the course of time it all came true. Amador died and Germain followed him as spiritual, instead of temporal, head of his well-loved city.

He was a great missionary and a great man. Austere in his personal life, yet compassionate and understanding with others, he carried his faith as if it were a great light. He went to England to convert the heathen there and the famous battle of the Picts and Scots is credited to his memory. It was Easter and the enemy was approaching in great numbers. Germain told his small army of converts to cast aside their arms and, chanting "Alleluia," to advance without fear. They did so and the opposing force, hearing the volume of victorious song, turned and fled in complete rout.

The tomb of this saint is as plain as even he could have wished. As we see it now, it was built as a thank-offering by Conrad, uncle of Charles the Bald. He had had a serious eye-trouble, which the application of herbs growing on the grave of Germain completely cured. Many other miracles are told of St. Germain, both during his life and after his demise. At the head of his last resting place is a little grated opening called his confessional. Through the centuries pilgrims have come to whisper through it their sins, their hopes or their fears, confident that his ears are as attentive and as sympathetic in death as they were in life.

When Sens and Auxerre were joined into one diocese, the cathedral of the latter became of necessity a parish church. It was built in less than fifty years, during the early part of the sixteenth century, and — as always happens when the period of construction is so short — the style is unusually pure. It is not alone Gothic, but it is the Gothic of that particular section of the country and of that particular epoch. If one may criticize a thing as lovely as this church of St. Étienne, it is a little too perfect, a little too unswerving from a definite model. One misses the happy accidents of change, the pleasant variations which the passage of time and fluctuating taste must bring. Yet it is a good fault after all, there is room in the world for more perfection.

The south tower unfortunately was never completed. Had it been, the façade would rank, I believe, with the great ones of France. As it is, there is one undeviating line from the southern eaves of the roof, up the steep pediment to the ridge, and up to the topmost corner of the northern tower. This is hard and graceless and gives the effect of an uncompromising triangle.

The proportions of the façade are otherwise fine. It is covered by a mass of delicate detail — canopies and pedestals of such exquisite fineness that one regrets especially the statues intended for them, yet never completed. The existing tower is strong and dignified and the portals, less mutilated than most at the time of the Revolution, are really lovely.

The interior is so majestic, so pure and aloof, that the account I had recently read of an ancient ceremony which used to take place there seemed doubly incongruous. In the early Church there were various practices which have long since disappeared from use, and some almost from memory. There were many in which a form of religious dance was enacted, surely a survival of ancient pagan rites. In the Cathedral of Auxerre the strangest ceremony was called that of the " pelota." I do not know the connection between it and the ancient, but still very much alive, Spanish game of that name, though the two must have been of identical origin. In this case a newly appointed canon presented a sphere whose size is unknown save that it is described as too large to be held in one hand, yet small enough that two hands might stop its flight. This was offered to the oldest dignitary of the chapter, who received it standing before the altar. He then took the hand of the canon upon his right and began to dance, upon which the other members joined in. After that came vespers, then a solemn supper at which were read aloud extracts from religious books. It was all very serious, there was nothing even remotely gay about the ceremony.

We left Auxerre with the feeling that it was repeating in reverse the life of its patron saint. He had started on a frivolous career which later became renowned for its austerity, while his city has lived through centuries of worthy works and is only lately turning its thoughts to more worldly things. In spite of tourists and blaring motor-cars, of hotels whose only thought is the possible financial response of each traveler, and of souvenir shops and signs, yet the beauty of the city, the endless historical associations, and a sincere religious foundation, are under it all — only a little blurred by the surface aspects of a modern commercial world.

LAON

LAON was the end of yet one more European summer for us; the leaden clouds, the drizzling rain and the tragic associations of this war-ravaged section, reflected somberly that mood of regret which the completion of any happy period must engender in us, no matter how much joy the immediate future seems to hold. We had heard, often and enthusiastically, of the beauty of this cathedral, and by rights we should have been anticipating our visit to it with the keenest pleasure; but instead, our thoughts were backward turned and sorrowing for the happy, roaming days so nearly over. Wise Fate, who believes in the inestimable value of surprise, cured us of all repining by treating us to a final experience so replete with beauty, and so unusual in character, as to make it in every respect a culminating point.

From the flat plain from which all trace of strife has been obliterated by the healing covering of new crops and by lines of young but growing trees, the ridge which is Laon rises steeply. Its sides are dotted with the gray houses of the old town whose weathered walls and roofs, slate-covered or with tiles neutral toned by time, form a unified mass. Above, the undulating line of the old fortified wall encircles as by a stone ribbon the central portion, the last stronghold, the old city.

At the end of this enclosure, the one-time cathedral of Notre Dame lifts its five towers sharply against the sky. So close was it built to the edge of the eminence on which it stands, that its foundations must strike down almost parallel to the mounting side of the hill, while, seen from below, one feels the continuity of that rising line which nature began and which man completed so harmoniously in the soaring mass of the church.

There are some happenings in life which enrich one's garnered store of remembered beauty, not alone by the quality of the object seen but even more so by the essence of it, filtered through a sympathetic mind. Such an experience was ours at Laon, where we tested and verified Corot's saying that " Art is Nature seen through a human soul."

Perhaps, if I had known this church of Notre Dame under different conditions, it might have lived in my memory as one with an unrivaled situation and many unusual features, yet which also had certain architectural defects of which

I should always have been conscious. As it is, visualized through eyes prejudiced by concentrated affection, interpreted by one who had studied it under all conditions and lived with it through a period of intimate years, I feel as reluctant to criticize it adversely as I would be to point out irregularities in a well-loved face. And it all happened this way.

A violent thunderstorm having cleared the air of steady rain and brought about a day of brilliant sunshine interrupted only by an occasional heavy, shower-laden cloud, J. T. took the car for protection against the latter possibility and wound a steep way up to the summit, to a vantage point upon the old Chemin de Ronde. So — thinking that a climb up the spiral tower staircase would be enough of that kind of exercise for one day — the Younger Generation and I avoided the three hundred and sixty steps which join the upper and lower towns and which the hardy natives use as casually as we a level street, and took the trusty tram which doggedly grips its racked third rail and grinds a noisy but restful way upwards. We arrived at the Hotel de Ville, its façade pockmarked with dark shrapnel scars, then a short walk brought us out upon the "place" before the cathedral. Quite aside from personal prejudice, it is a lovely and unusual building. This western wall, with its two square towers to the north and south and its three portals, is neither Rheims nor Notre Dame de Paris, but suggestive of each. It lacks the delicacy of the one and the strength of the other, but in its own way it is a beautiful thing.

On entering, we found ourselves in an interior in which the feeling of light and spaciousness dominated. The plan of the church is cruciform, with a rectangular eastern end, in the high wall of which are three deep-set windows of rich stained glass, and above them a beautiful rose embodying a feature which I never remember seeing elsewhere. Whereas in most windows of this type the glazing is set with about the same depth of muntin on the inside as is found on the outside, here the projection is all on the exterior, the interior being flush with the glass. The theory was advanced to us that this stone was originally painted the deep blue found in the background of the very beautiful surrounding glass, in order to give an effect of a single uninterrupted area of color. I doubt if the result was very successful, as it seems not to have been repeated, and certainly the dark outlines of the stone tracery, intensifying the brilliant tones of the jewel-like medallions, could hardly be improved upon.

The central aisle of the nave is unusually wide, with a deep triforium of high arches which are in turn surmounted by an arcade, and still above that are large windows in the clerestory through the plain panes of which the strong sun streams unimpeded. These upper motives are carried along the nave, along the sides of the wide transepts and up the length of the apse to the eastern end, causing the effect which we first noticed of size, of delicacy of construction and of brilliant light.

The interior is refreshingly bare of church furniture. In the fifteenth and sixteenth centuries the lateral chapels were enclosed by charming stone Renaissance screens, which effectually hide the various altars and form a homogeneous line of sculpture. In the body of the church are found only the bare necessities, the warden's pew, a pulpit and some meager rows of chairs to break up the vast emptiness. This church of Notre Dame lacks more than the pleasant absence of ugly modern statues and tawdry furnishings, it also lacks its one-time importance as a cathedral and lives, now a simple parish church, in the sad magnificence of splendid memories.

It was a mighty see and its bishops were rich, powerful, and sometimes unscrupulous. The burning of the Episcopal Palace in 1111 showed to what lengths the townspeople carried their resentment of the tyranny which had destroyed their Charter of Rights. Unfortunately, this revolt went farther than they had planned. The inexorable flames spread to the nearby church, the wooden roofing of that period caught and burned so fiercely that the entire building was destroyed and even the costly gifts, brought through the years by kings and princes, melted in the heat or were irretrievably damaged. The new cathedral rose from this ruin ; eighty years saw its virtual completion, a significant factor in the unity and purity of its style. Its power continued and its treasury was replenished by new and splendid tributes, and all went as smoothly as those turbulent centuries permitted, until the Revolution, with its wave of destruction, took from it all but its beautiful structural shell. And when this iconoclastic tide receded, Notre Dame found itself despoiled also of its bishop and under the spiritual power of Soissons. Its final reverses came about during the last war, when from 1914 to 1918 the enemy army held the town and stabled its horses in the white purity of the nave. The very stones must have cried out against the desecration.

On our first visit to the church we roamed about alone through this vast interior, peering between the carved pillars of the chapel screens at worn sculptured fragments, collected and put there for safe-keeping when newer ones replaced them, or gazing up at the grouped heads or single figures which act as brackets or corbels under the upper columns. Our straying steps finally brought us to the sacristy, opening out from the ambulatory. Permission to enter having

LAON

LAON
NOTRE DAME DE LAON
Size of the original etching, 13⅞ inches by 9⅜ inches

Notre Dame de Laon

John Taylor Arms 1919

been granted by a black-smocked, skull-capped sacristan, we did so and began examining the Brussels tapestries hanging about the walls. The story of them is that of Jacob and Rachel, one seldom represented and quite rightly so, it seems to me. Why a pair so obviously dishonest should have become venerated ancestors in the eyes of even the most credulous of descendants, has always been a mystery to me; and when I saw Rachel depicted in one tapestry as furtively and hurriedly packing the dearly loved idols of her father, I felt the common vulgarity of the tale even more strongly. The apprehensive stealth of her gesture and pose was admirably portrayed, even though one deplored her lack of character and the mean motive behind her actions.

The sacristan—a person educated far beyond his position, with a scholar's stoop and the visionary eye of an idealist—evidently decided that he might show us a treasure or two without feeling too much that he was casting the proverbial unappreciated pearls; so he condescended to explain a story here, or show us a sacred relic there, warming to his subject as he did so. The pride of the collection was a very old painting of the Miraculous Face, that imprint said to have been made upon the cloth with which St. Veronica wiped the face of Christ as He passed her on the road to Calvary. It is curiously painted, with letters said by an expert to date it from the tenth century or before. It was given by Urban IV to his sister, abbess of a convent at Laon where he had established her because of his affection for this city in which he had spent a part of his youth. He was certainly a canon here and he is also claimed as a cathedral choir-boy, though Troyes, the city of his birth, makes the same assertion and with perhaps even greater reason.

By this time our interesting guide had become enthusiastic and, quite ignoring a hopeful group waiting to climb the tower, he started us on one of the most intensive and absorbing tours that it has ever been my good fortune to enjoy. First he conducted us to the more or less conventional things; to see the chapel of fragments where a Crucifixion, mutilated by the Revolutionists, still remains more beautiful and dramatic in pose and drapery than most complete works of art; then to study the apsidal windows with their stories of the childhood of Jesus, of St. Stephen — first Christian martyr — and of St. Théophile, that contradictory person, who, having sold his soul to the devil, took the money thus evilly gained and built churches and did good works until the Virgin in a dream implored him to come back into the straight and narrow path. He wakened, the sinful pact was in his hand for him to destroy. This he did and after years of virtue he ultimately died in high honor and great sanctity. We also went out through the Chapter Room into a space too small to call a court, where, standing on a heap of coal and rubbish, we gazed up at a window hidden by this newer building except from this one point. It was of the curious design found also in the bit of remaining cloister and in the chapel of the fonts — a small rose of heavy, primitive tracery with a circle of round apertures surrounding it.

At intervals the sacristan would pause and, casting a severe look at us from under shaggy eyebrows, would ask us if we had seen enough or would we care to see yet more beauties? What he really meant was — were we capable of appreciating still greater things — though he was too courteous to phrase it that way. At our continued enthusiasm he unbent more and more, then, excusing himself, went to sound the chimes. With practiced hand he pulled the cord which rings the bell in the tower high overhead. He first rang twelve times, in groups of three, then thirty-three separate and distinct strokes. We counted mechanically as we waited, and puzzled over the number without success until he elucidated it for us. The four groups were for the quarter hours passed since the last ringing, and the thirty-three stood for each year of Christ's life on earth.

" It is the hour of dinner, do you mind waiting?" he asked abruptly, in itself an extraordinary question for a Frenchman to propound. " No? Then we shall all dine at the same table, on the beauty of a lovely church!" And with this poetic remark he led us up the stairs to the triforium above the nave. There I had a distinct surprise. In several churches recently seen — notably in Notre Dame at Caudebec — I had regretted the balustrade which joins the lower portions of the columns and slender piers of the gallery, and so cuts the graceful height of the arches by about a third. Here, when seen from below, this balustrade was delightfully absent; but when we came out upon the broad upper gallery above the aisle of the nave, bounded on one side by the southern wall and on the other by a line of columns unconnected by any form of railing between, I looked with a giddy sense of insecurity down to the pavement so far below me and felt that there was much to be said in favor of the other treatment. I never quite became accustomed to that utterly unprotected feeling, and perhaps the very instability of it added to the dizzy effect of being suspended in the air in the midst of loveliness.

We walked the length of the nave along this aërial aisle, with something of interest to be seen every foot of the way. At the crossing we turned sharply to the right, then out over the wide open platform above the southern portal, along the eastern side of the transept, and up the length of the apse to the great

rose window, which we could then almost touch. It was here, above the choir,
that we saw the faint suggestion of a curve in the abacus of a column, indicating
the old shape of the original rounded apse before the deep rectangular one was
added.

The carving too showed, in refinement and design, a subtle difference
between the old world and the new. There were chapels on this level, one with
a strawberry leaf motive in the ceiling which was perfect and exquisite to a
degree. Nearby a tiny head served as a key to the vaulting, the only woman's
head so used in any church, they say. And everywhere were vistas across the
church to the opposite gallery, through arches and yet more arches into seemingly limitless space.

We went through doors with " No admission" firmly chalked upon them,
up steps, down steps, and out upon an open space beside the great roof. This
was the base of one of the incompleted towers, of which seven were planned
and only five were built. From here we were shown a line of gargoyles depicting the seven deadly sins, six of them large, strong figures; only Avarice was
half-size, vividly suggesting the shrunken meanness of its nature.

And still we climbed, this time up one of the west towers. These are rather
curious in their construction. They are each composed of four openwork buttresses, joined by louvered sides. In one of these turrets was a tiny spiral staircase, up which we boldly started. All went well as long as we were in the solid
base, but when we reached the level of the roof we came to the part where the
open arches began. Our left hands desperately clutched the central shaft, worn
smooth and slippery by just such contacts; on our right the slender columns
and tracery of these unglassed windows offered scant protection, compared to
the airy nothingness of the spaces between. We hastily averted our eyes from
dizzy glimpses of the country below us, and with set jaws stepped, or crawled,
our upward way. It was not far in reality, but it seemed long until we emerged
upon the blessed safety of a flat, parapetted roof which offered a view worth
the perilous climb and much, much more. Immediately below us was the
church with its great roof and rising towers, the adjoining one so close that we
felt a friendly nearness to the giant oxen on the corners, their great heads thrust
forward. They commemorate the patient beasts who voluntarily dragged the
stone, load by load, from the far-off quarry, that the cathedral might be built.
Another legend says that when a weight became too great for even these strong
and willing beasts to haul up the steep roads which even now curve and zigzag on the precipitous hill, a monster ox appeared and, joining his limitless

strength to theirs, pulled the inert, ponderous mass to the summit with miraculous ease, then disappeared. We looked down also on the roof of the one-time Episcopal Palace, separated from the church by a little garden, nearby which stood the ancient Hotel Dieu. Was there ever a lovelier name than this designation of a hospital for the very poor? To the west lay the old town on its steep-sided ridge, the tortuous streets so narrow that they hardly broke up its homogeneous mass. We could see the church of St. Martin, badly injured during the war, although the townspeople, with a natural reserve born of suffering and the need to forget, belittle the damage to that building and all others. Our sacristan told us that one bomb fell in the " place" before the cathedral but miraculously exploded away from the building, leaving it untouched. Others admit, however, that some harm was done. Around the town the wall dipped and rose as it followed the natural contours of the ground. It curved out and about, with a curious leaning arch at the farther end ; then back again, seeming to hold the clustered houses yet more closely. The great railroad junction, with the modern red-roofed section of the town about it, seemed symbolic of new importance, for this is the only large town for many miles. The view appeared endless, over country always historic and recently tragically so. A line of young trees in the distance marked the Chemin des Dames, perhaps the most hotly contested road of the World War. Almost indistinguishable spots in the distance were once prosperous villages, but are now formless heaps of ruins. Already so much has been done to obliterate all traces of disaster that soon this countryside will look as peaceful and undramatic as the Field of Waterloo.

Railway-tracks, roads, and lines of telegraph poles stretched in every direction. It was as if we stood in the center of the world and all things converged towards us. Once pilgrims came from distant places with Laon as a religious objective, kings sent or brought their gifts to the powerful archbishop whose rule was temporal as well as spiritual, and merchants came and traded here. Those days are gone, yet the long lines of contact bring the world still to this rather remote town and lend it a different and a modern importance.

I thought, as I stood on that high tower, that town and experience alike made of Laon more than an individual for me, rather a symbol of France and our feeling for it. It was a storied spot, yet little enough known to give a joyous sense of discovery. It was beautiful and worthy of much study and it offered an opportunity to realize the sensitiveness to loveliness, the courteous coöperation and the rare quality of educated appreciation found at its best in the French provincial, however humble his station in life. It was the last stop of a perfect summer, but those long converging lines stood, to me, for the paths which here in France lead always to beauty.